DATE			

Abortion

[OPPOSING
VIEWPOINTS®
DIGESTS]

Books in the
Opposing Viewpoints Digests Series:

The American Revolution

Animal Rights

The Bill of Rights

Biomedical Ethics

Child Abuse

The Civil War

The Death Penalty

Drugs and Sports

Endangered Species

The Environment

The Fall of the Roman Empire

Gangs

The Great Depression

Gun Control

The 1960s

Slavery

Teen Violence

Abortion

STEPHEN CURRIE

Greenhaven Press, Inc., San Diego, California

Library of Congress Cataloging-in-Publication Data

Currie, Stephen, 1960–
    Abortion / Stephen Currie
        p.   cm. — (Opposing viewpoints digests)
    Includes bibliographical references and index.
    Summary: Presents opposing viewpoints on abortion, discussing such issues as morality, legality, restriction of abortion rights, and research using aborted fetal tissue.
        ISBN 0-7377-0229-X (lib. bdg. : alk. paper). —
        ISBN 0-7377-0228-1 (pbk. : alk. paper)
    1. Abortion—Juvenile literature. 2. Pro-choice movement—Juvenile literature. 3. Pro-life movement—Juvenile literature.
    [1. Abortion.] I. Title. II. Series
    HQ767.C87   2000
    363.46 21—dc21   99-042785

Cover Photo: © Bob Daemmrich/Uniphoto
AP/Wide World Photos: 20
© 1995 Jerome Friar, Impact Visuals: 27
© 1993 David Rae Morris, Impact Visuals: 41

CONTENTS

Foreword   6

Introduction: The Increasingly Complex and
    Emotional Debate over Abortion   8

Chapter 1: Is Abortion Immoral?
1. Abortion Is Murder   24
2. Abortion Is Not Murder   30

Chapter 2: Should Abortion Be Legal?
1. Abortion Should Be Legal   37
2. Abortion Should Only Be Legal in
   Certain Cases   44
3. Abortion Should Be Illegal   50

Chapter 3: Should Abortion Rights Be Restricted?
1. Partial-Birth Abortions Should Be Banned   61
2. Partial-Birth Abortions Should Not Be Banned   66
3. Parental Consent Laws Are Necessary   72
4. Parental Consent Laws Have Harmful Effects   78

**Chapter 4: Is Research Using Aborted Fetal
    Tissue Ethical?**
1. Fetal Tissue Research Is Unnecessary and Immoral   85
2. Fetal Tissue Research Is Ethical and Will Save Lives   92

Study Questions   99
Appendix A: Facts About Abortion   101
Appendix B: Excerpts from Related Documents   102
Organizations to Contact   110
For Further Reading   115
Works Consulted   116
Index   121
About the Author   127

FOREWORD

The only way in which a human being can make some approach to knowing the whole of a subject is by hearing what can be said about it by persons of every variety of opinion and studying all modes in which it can be looked at by every character of mind. No wise man ever acquired his wisdom in any mode but this.

—John Stuart Mill

Today, young adults are inundated with a wide variety of points of view on an equally wide spectrum of subjects. Often overshadowing traditional books and newspapers as forums for these views are a host of broadcast, print, and electronic media, including television news and entertainment programs, talk shows, and commercials; radio talk shows and call-in lines; movies, home videos, and compact discs; magazines and supermarket tabloids; and the increasingly popular and influential Internet.

For teenagers, this multiplicity of sources, ideas, and opinions can be both positive and negative. On the one hand, a wealth of useful, interesting, and enlightening information is readily available virtually at their fingertips, underscoring the need for teens to recognize and consider a wide range of views besides their own. As Mark Twain put it, "It were not best that we should all think alike; it is difference of opinion that makes horse races." On the other hand, the range of opinions on a given subject is often too wide to absorb and analyze easily. Trying to keep up with, sort out, and form personal opinions from such a barrage can be daunting for anyone, let alone young people who have not yet acquired effective critical judgment skills.

Moreover, to the task of evaluating this assortment of impersonal information, many teenagers bring firsthand experience of serious and emotionally charged social and health problems, including divorce, family violence, alcoholism and drug abuse, rape, unwanted pregnancy, the spread of AIDS, and eating disorders. Teens are often forced to deal with these problems before they are capable of objective opinion based on reason and judgment. All too often, teens' response to these deep personal issues is impulsive rather than carefully considered.

Greenhaven Press's Opposing Viewpoints Digests are designed to aid in examining important current issues in a way that develops critical thinking and evaluating skills. Each book presents thought-provoking argument and stimulating debate on a single issue. By examining an issue from many different points of view, readers come to realize its complexity and acknowledge the validity of opposing opinions. This insight is especially helpful in writing reports, research papers, and persuasive essays, when students must competently address common objections and controversies related to their topic. In addition, examination of the diverse mix of opinions in each volume challenges readers to question their own strongly held opinions and assumptions. While the point of such examination is not to change readers' minds, examining views that oppose their own will certainly deepen their own knowledge of the issue and help them realize exactly why they hold the opinion they do.

The Opposing Viewpoints Digests offer a number of unique features that sharpen young readers' critical thinking and reading skills. To assure an appropriate and consistent reading level for young adults, all essays in each volume are written by a single author. Each essay heavily quotes readable primary sources that are fully cited to allow for further research and documentation. Thus, primary sources are introduced in a context to enhance comprehension.

In addition, each volume includes extensive research tools. A section containing relevant source material includes interviews, excerpts from original research, and the opinions of prominent spokespersons. A "facts about" section allows students to peruse relevant facts and statistics; these statistics are also fully cited, allowing students to question and analyze the credibility of the source. Two bibliographies, one for young adults and one listing the author's sources, are also included; both are annotated to guide student research. Finally, a comprehensive index allows students to scan and locate content efficiently.

Greenhaven's Opposing Viewpoints Digests, like Greenhaven's higher level and critically acclaimed Opposing Viewpoints Series, have been developed around the concept that an awareness and appreciation for the complexity of seemingly simple issues is particularly important in a democratic society. In a democracy, the common good is often, and very appropriately, decided by open debate of widely varying views. As one of our democracy's greatest advocates, Thomas Jefferson, observed, "Difference of opinion leads to inquiry, and inquiry to truth." It is to this principle that Opposing Viewpoints Digests are dedicated.

The Increasingly Complex and Emotional Debate over Abortion

Today few debates in American politics and society are as complex as the debate over abortion. The question of abortion encompasses many different issues, from the biological question of when life begins to the social question of the quality of an unwanted child's life; from the legal question of whether some, or all, abortions should be outlawed to the ethical question of whether a rape victim may be required to bear her attacker's child.

Because of the complexity of the debate, positions on abortion are unusually polarized. Indeed, people on different sides of the issue may not only dispute each other's facts and disagree about what is to be done but also argue about what terms to use in describing abortion, abortion providers, abortion procedures, and each other. The result is a highly charged and extremely contentious debate.

History

Abortion has been known since ancient times. Women in virtually all cultures have used it as a method of birth control, re-

gardless of whether the culture officially permitted it. Over many centuries, women wishing to terminate a pregnancy have drunk mildly poisonous liquids, rubbed certain herbs on their stomachs, or attempted to pierce their wombs with sharp objects. They may have acted alone, or they may have had help. Sometimes these methods of abortion indeed destroyed the fetus. Sometimes, however, the woman succeeded only in hurting herself. At best, abortion was a hit-or-miss proposition in which the stakes for the pregnant woman were quite high.

In the middle of the nineteenth century, however, this situation began to change. As medical technology and knowledge increased, so did the options available to abortion-seeking women. Over the decades, operating techniques grew refined enough to allow a doctor or a reasonably skilled layman to surgically remove a fetus from the womb. While this procedure almost always resulted in the successful termination of the pregnancy, many of the old risks for the woman remained. Until the development of antibiotics in the 1940s, the death rate among women from abortions was quite high.

Cultural Responses to Abortion

Different cultures have had different views of abortion. Many have accepted it, at times even encouraging women to abort. These peoples have seen abortion as a reasonable method of population control, desirable during times of famine or other stress on their people. Other cultures, however, have been much less accepting of abortion: They have set up elaborate lists of reasons and times when having an abortion was appropriate and when it was not. Still others have consistently frowned on the practice or banned it entirely.

At different times, Western societies have taken all of these stances on the abortion question. Abortions were permitted by English common law at the time of the first European settlement, as long as the abortion was performed before "quickening"—the moment in pregnancy, usually occurring around four months after conception, when the mother first notices fetal movement. This custom, in turn, was adopted by the American colonies. Exactly how common abortion was in colonial times is impossible to know, but most experts believe that it was far from rare. Certainly, many newspapers of the time ran advertisements for abortion-inducing drugs.

English common law was not the only Western institution that accepted abortion in certain cases. So, too, did many churches. Between the fifth and nineteenth centuries, for example, the official teachings of the Roman Catholic Church nearly always permitted at least some early abortions—or, at the very least, punished early abortion much less seriously than ones carried out later in the pregnancy. Abortion "does not count as killing," wrote St. Jerome, "until the individual elements have acquired their external appearance and their limbs."[1] St. Augustine, St. Thomas Aquinas, and Pope Innocent III were among Catholic thinkers who agreed with St.

Jerome, as long as abortion was performed within the first 40 to 90 days of pregnancy. Pope Gregory XIV, who ruled at the end of the sixteenth century, extended the limit to 116 days. Abortions performed before that time carried no penalty at all.

Nor was acceptance of abortion limited to Catholics. Most Protestant denominations have traditionally held more or less the same opinion. Official Methodist and Episcopal church publications were among the colonial American newspapers happy to accept abortion-drug advertisements. With religious leaders willing to accept or at least overlook early-term abortions, abortion was not the moral issue it would later become.

The permissive approach to abortion began to change, though, in the nineteenth century. Exactly why these changes occurred is unclear. Some commentators have suggested that the changes were sparked by greater concern for public health; while abortion was becoming less risky for women, it was not by any means safe. Some scientists, too, were beginning to question whether there was a significant difference between the earlier and later stages of fetal development. Others attribute the shifting attitudes to "a Victorian obsession to discourage illicit sexual conduct"[2] by punishing women who chose to have extramarital sex. Finally, anti-immigrant sentiment played a role in the United States as well. Many people of Protestant descent feared that Catholic immigrants from Ireland and southern Europe would soon outnumber native-born Americans since it was believed that these immigrants had fewer abortions. Access to abortion, some worried, would hasten the decline of what the native-born liked to call "good Anglo-Saxon stock."[3]

Whatever the reasons for this change in attitude may have been, laws certainly began to change as a result. One by one, U.S. state legislatures began to make intentional abortion unlawful, regardless of how far along the pregnancy had advanced. New York banned abortion in 1828, though the new law called for stiffer penalties for abortions performed after quickening than for earlier abortions. By 1860 most states had similar laws on the books, as did a number of European nations. In 1869 Pope Pius IX officially changed Catholic doctrine to ban all abortions performed at any time for any reason. Even the American Medical Association, later a strong supporter of abortion rights, opposed access to abortion during the 1860s. By the mid–nineteenth century, abortion was typically regarded as both criminal and immoral.

Abortion in the Twentieth Century

The fact that abortion was considered unethical and illegal did not stop American women from obtaining the procedure. Some state laws still permitted abortions if they were performed for certain medical or psychological reasons. And illegal abortion was a frequent choice as well, especially as medical advances made it increasingly safer to women and more certain to destroy the fetus. Estimates of the number of illegal abortions performed each year during the 1960s, for instance, range from a low of about two hundred thousand up to one million. As long as women felt that carrying a particular pregnancy to term would be harmful in some way—harmful to their health, harmful to their futures, harmful because of the possibilities of birth defects or bearing an unloved and unwanted child—abortion continued.

However, little attempt was made to reform the laws against abortion until relatively recently. In 1959 the American Law Institute (ALI) produced a model abortion law that allowed abortion in the cases of rape, birth defects, or a generalized concern about the mother's physical and mental health. Several states took the opportunity to write these exceptions into their own laws, although pro-life legislators argued that the physical and mental health exceptions, in particular, were open to interpretation and would inevitably be used to justify abortion on demand.

In 1969 the California Supreme Court went even further. It ruled that the state's antiabortion law, as written, was unconstitutional. The law was rewritten, but the damage was done. Later that same year the abortion regulations of Washington,

D.C., were overturned by a court. This time no new replacement law was passed, and the District of Columbia had ceased to outlaw most abortions.

Change was on the way. The next few years saw a number of referenda on repealing abortion laws in various states. Most failed, but some came close to succeeding, and the fact that abortion was now open to public debate was a significant change from previous years. Reformers took heart. They began a spirited public opinion campaign in several states, stressing, as one researcher writes,

> the high number of illegal abortions, the fact that poor women were being discriminated against [by high costs and the lack of medical insurance], the need for abortion where contraception had failed, the fact that unwanted pregnancies led to social problems, and the need for population control.[4]

In 1970 these arguments took root in Hawaii. The legislature repealed state abortion laws, and the Catholic governor of the state signed the bill. For the first time in years, an American state had repealed its law forbidding abortion. Alaska followed suit; so did Washington and New York. Meanwhile, other states, including New Jersey, Wisconsin, and Kansas, were continuing to adopt the ALI's model laws or were having their own restrictions declared unconstitutional by the courts. And the federal Commission on Population and the American Future weighed in with a report that recommended "the liberalization of state abortion laws along the lines of the New York statute, the most liberal of all the new laws."[5]

The push to legalize abortion was growing in strength. Clearly many women wanted to choose the procedure; in the two and a half years between July 1970 and December 1972, more than three hundred thousand women from all across the country flocked to New York for legal abortions. Yet, at the same time, there was much opposition to new and liberalized abortion laws. Despite the number of out-of-state women who came to New

York for abortions, few people outside of urban centers, the Northeast, and part of the West Coast publicly accepted the notion that abortion was anything other than the murder of a human being. Feminists and liberals who opposed restrictions on abortion were themselves opposed by most self-described conservatives, many political moderates, and the official teachings of the Roman Catholic Church and many Protestant denominations. Even to the reformers, it seemed that obtaining universal abortion rights would be a long and slow process.

Roe v. Wade

Then, in 1973, an important abortion case came before the U.S. Supreme Court. Norma McCorvey, a resident of Dallas, had sought an abortion but was prevented from obtaining one legally by Texas's antiabortion law. Rather than go to a state where abortion was legal or undergo an illegal procedure, McCorvey—backed by reformers looking for a test case—decided to fight. Using the pseudonym "Jane Roe," she sued Henry Wade, the district attorney of her county, on the grounds that the statute violated the U.S. Constitution.

Roe v. Wade wound its way slowly through the legal system and eventually to the Supreme Court. In a surprising 7-2 decision, the Court ruled in favor of McCorvey, thus sweeping down antiabortion laws all across the country. The reason for the decision rested partly on the concept of the right of privacy. Although the right of privacy is not explicitly mentioned anywhere in the Constitution, it nevertheless has been cited many times by jurists as a basic and important right of Americans. The right of privacy, argued Justice Harry Blackmun, included family issues such as when and whether to bear children, decisions that Blackmun believed were not of the government's concern. In particular, Blackmun wrote, the right of privacy was "broad enough to encompass a woman's decision whether or not to terminate her pregnancy."[6]

The Court's decision also rested partly on the fact that abortion had become a good deal safer over the years. When the original antiabortion laws were passed, Blackmun reasoned, the states could justify banning abortion because a woman's life was seriously endangered by the procedure: In sum, the laws were to protect the pregnant woman from a dangerous operation. Medical advances, however, had changed matters. By the 1970s, early abortion was very safe as medical procedures went—statistically safer, in fact, than childbirth—so very few women were in danger of risking their health or lives by undergoing the operation. Thus, the state could no longer claim it had women's best interests at heart by banning early abortions.

Limits on Abortion

However, the Supreme Court did not entirely abandon the fetus. While sidestepping the question of when life actually begins, Blackmun did not permit abortion on demand for anyone at any time. Instead, he set different standards for abortions at different times during pregnancy. Medical science had typically divided pregnancy into three three-month stages, or trimesters, and Blackmun used these divisions to determine what would be permissible.

During the first trimester of pregnancy, the Court ruled, abortion essentially could not be regulated by the states at all—it was a personal and private matter between a woman and her doctor. During the second trimester, however, there were legitimate concerns about the woman's health in undergoing abortion. Thus, states could set policies that made it more difficult to get second trimester abortions, though states were not allowed to forbid it altogether.

The third trimester was a different situation. Here, Blackmun wrote, the fetus was well enough developed that its rights needed to be taken into account as well. As he put it, "The state in promoting its interest in the potentiality of human life may, if it chooses, regulate, and even proscribe abortion except where it is necessary . . . for the preservation of the life or health of the mother."[7] This permission to ban abortions only during the final three months of pregnancy was small comfort to the forces opposed to reform, but at least, they reasoned, the Court had not struck down all abortion-related legislation, as some activists had urged it to do.

Roe v. Wade has seen plenty of challenges since 1973. Several of these court cases have established that states may limit abortions in certain ways. States may, for example, require a woman to wait twenty-four hours for an abortion after letting a doctor or clinic know of her intent. Many states have passed laws requiring teenagers to tell their parents that they want an abortion or, in some cases, to obtain parental permission; these laws, too, have been upheld. In a somewhat different vein, the federal and some state governments have passed regulations making it difficult or impossible for certain government-funded clinics to perform abortions or even discuss the subject with their patients. The essence of *Roe v. Wade*, however—that women have a constitutional right to abortion—remains unchanged.

Continuing Controversy

That is not to say that controversy over abortion has lessened. Indeed, abortion is still a loaded issue in America today. In

some ways, it is perhaps more contentious than ever. At the root of the quarrel is a fundamental difference in people's perception of what abortion means. For those who would like to ban abortion altogether, abortion boils down to a matter of life and death: With an abortion, the fetus dies; without an abortion, the fetus may continue to live. This viewpoint is reflected in language, too. People on the side of the fetus in this debate call themselves "pro-life" or "right-to-life" and characterize their opponents as "proabortion," "pro-death," "anti-life," or "baby killers."

Opponents of pro-lifers, however, reject the notion that abortion is about killing. They frame the issue, instead, as a question of a pregnant woman's right to control her body. They argue that a fetus is a collection of cells, nothing more than a *potential* life. To them, the argument is about choice: A pregnant woman must have the ability to terminate her pregnancy if she so chooses. Thus, supporters of legal abortion prefer to call themselves "pro-choice" and refer to their opponents as "antichoice," "antiwoman," "right-wing extremists," or "fanatics."

Language differences extend even further than this. A place where abortions are available is called a "clinic" by one side, an "abortuary" or "abortion mill" by the other. Pro-choicers emphasize the safe, medical nature of abortion with their phrase. Going to have an abortion is not much different from going to have any other relatively minor same-day surgery. The pro-life phrase *abortion mill*, however, conjures up warehouses and factories where women are sent along an assembly line by cold, uncaring workers, and the connection of the word *abortuary* with *mortuary* reminds readers that abortion results in a death.

Similarly, the pro-choice forces speak of the "procedure" and of abortion "providers," while some right-to-lifers talk instead of "child killing." More recently, a late-term abortion procedure widely known as "partial-birth abortion" has moved to the forefront of the controversy. The term *partial-birth abortion* is the right-to-lifers'. They find the phrase descriptive of a process in which the fetus is delivered partway before it dies. Pro-choice groups, however, dislike the phrase and feel it is misleading. They accuse pro-lifers of lumping any number of other abortion procedures in with this one and refer, instead, to "so-called partial-birth abortion." The differences in terminology reflect differences in ideology and make it hard for opponents to communicate effectively with each other.

Ambivalence

Conflicting court decisions and the mishmash of state regulations have increased debate, too. Neither side has been very happy with most judicial decisions. Right-to-lifers mourn the fact that *Roe v. Wade* is still the law of the land; pro-choicers dislike the many obstacles that courts are willing to allow. Like the courts, the American people seem ambivalent: ready to accept some limitations on abortion yet unwilling to ban access to it completely; uncomfortable with abortion's destruction of a fetus while not considering abortion exactly the same as murder; critical of the idea of unrestricted abortion on demand while supporting the idea that some abortions are justified.

Opinion polls routinely demonstrate the truth of this. Although the results of surveys vary according to the exact wording of the poll questions, most surveys show the largest mass of Americans to be solidly in the middle. In a 1992 survey, for instance, 31 percent of respondents said that abortion should "always" be legal, while 14 percent replied "never"; over half of those polled, however, hedged by replying that abortion should be legal "under certain circumstances."[8] Other polls have come up with somewhat different numbers and ratios, but as a general rule the majority opts for a middle position.

Apparent contradictions reign, too. According to a 1981 survey, for example, 67 percent of those polled believed that at least some abortions ought to remain legal, but 56 percent stated that abortion was morally wrong. Clearly, a significant percentage of the respondents believed that abortion was immoral yet thought it ought to be legal—hardly a decision that either side would applaud. While both pro-choice and pro-life groups like to cite surveys that seem to support their point of view, most Americans are not entirely comfortable with the rhetoric and tactics of either side. The polls, instead of showing what the various sides would like to see, show that most Americans are somewhere in the ambivalent middle.

This ambivalence, in which neither side ever can quite grasp a clear upper hand, also serves to heighten tensions. When questions have gone unresolved for years, victory on even minor issues takes on special importance. Moreover, each side is constantly afraid that it may lose some of its authority after the next court decision, the next election, even the next opinion poll. Thus, both pro-choice and pro-life organizations work frantically to attract the mass of people in the middle by playing up their strengths and also by pointing out the other side's weaknesses, excesses, and inconsistencies.

Of course, as the years go by, the debate shifts. New scientific evidence sets arguments in new directions. A current topic is the fate of so-called abortion drugs, notably the French medication RU-486, which promises—or threatens, depending on the viewer's perspective—to make nonsurgical abortion possible. Another recent controversy involves using aborted fetuses for medical research—scientists say such research could save lives, but many believe that using fetal tissue in this way is unethical and might provide an incentive for women to have abortions.

Social conditions change, too, sparking new debate. In the years immediately after *Roe v. Wade*, for instance, there was little illegal protest by pro-life forces. Today, hundreds of incidents occur each year—from vandalism and scuffles during protests to shooting abortion providers—bringing up the question of whether this type of action is justifiable. The basic questions regarding abortion—whether it is murder, whether it ought to be legal, whether there are ever occasions when it can be justified—are still at the heart of the debate, but there are new questions to be asked, too.

Professor Emile-Etienne Beaulieu displays RU-486 pills, an abortion drug which he invented. Advances in medicine have further complicated the debate over abortion.

Types of Disagreements

The arguments stem from many different sources. Sometimes the sides do not agree on facts. Several studies, for example, have suggested that women who undergo abortions have a higher risk of getting breast cancer. Pro-life forces sometimes cite these studies as evidence that abortion is bad for a woman's health. Other researchers, however, have found no such link, and pro-choice forces have championed these studies instead. The furor over late-term partial-birth abortion is another good example of a debate in which the two sides do not accept the same definitions and information.

In most abortion-related issues, though, the difference is not so much facts as values and interpretation. A twenty-four-hour waiting period, pro-choicers argue, represents a huge burden for many women. It may make abortion especially difficult, if not impossible, for rural women, poor women, and those who wish to keep their decisions regarding abortion private. Pro-lifers respond that waiting periods serve to protect fetuses and their mothers from rash, hastily made decisions to abort, decisions that may well be regretted in the future. Both sides can legitimately claim that they have the best interests of women at heart. The question is not simply who is right, but what constitutes "best interests."

Whatever the cause of the disagreements, they are deeply rooted. Ethicists and politicians alike search for common ground between the pro-choice and pro-life forces. They fail more often than they succeed, for even the most reasonable of voices on both sides are often far apart. As long as some people decry abortion as baby killing and others talk about how legal abortion safeguards women's rights; as long as some believe that life begins at conception and others hold that the early fetus is very far from being a human; as long as some argue that nothing can outweigh the fetus's ultimate right to life and others assert that poverty, fragile mental health, or concern about fetal deformities all justify a woman in seeking to terminate her pregnancy, the debate surrounding abortion can only continue.

1. Quoted in "Past and Present Beliefs of the Christian Church on Abortion." www.religioustolerance.org/abo_hist.htm.
2. Marlena Sobel, "Abortion Myths," July 1994. www.berkshire.net/~ifas/fw/9407/myths.html.

3. Quoted in Alison Landes et al., eds., *Abortion: An Eternal Social and Moral Issue.* Wylie, TX: Information Plus, 1996, p. 8.

4. Colin Francome, *Abortion Freedom: A Worldwide Movement.* London: George Allen and Unwin, 1984, p. 115.

5. Quoted in Landes et al., *Abortion*, p. 11.

6. Quoted in Robert M. Baird and Stuart E. Rosenbaum, *The Ethics of Abortion.* Buffalo: Prometheus Books, 1993, p. 36.

7. Quoted in Baird and Rosenbaum, *The Ethics of Abortion*, p. 40.

8. Quoted in Landes et al., *Abortion*, p. 161.

CHAPTER 1

Is Abortion Immoral?

"When children are viciously killed, we call the act what it is: Murder. We must do the same for children who have yet to be born."

Abortion Is Murder

Abortion is the death of a person, a living human being distinct from any other individual on this planet. This fact may be inconvenient for those who would like to see abortion as a question of women's rights or a matter of individual conscience, but it is nonetheless undeniable. As the bumpersticker slogan reads, "Abortion stops a beating heart."[1] Aborting a fetus is not, as some would have it, equivalent to removing a tumor or a wart. It is far more serious. Plain and simple, abortion is murder.

Murder is the intentional killing of an innocent person, and abortion clearly fits all parts of the definition. First, an abortion is obviously intentional; women who have abortions make plans and appointments to kill their babies. Second, the fetus is clearly innocent. It can do no wrong and commit no crimes; it is not trying to hurt another person. Abortion is not the same as killing in self-defense, nor is it the same as capital punishment, each of which assumes that the one who dies is guilty of some great evil. Instead, it is the killing of an innocent—a fetus whose only goal is to be born.

And, third, a fetus is unquestionably a person. A small person, yes; a person restricted in space, true; a person who may not at first glance seem to fit the stereotypes of a person, to be sure. Nevertheless, a fetus *is* a person, a miraculous and wonderful living human being who must be protected, not killed. "The embryo," writes philosopher Roger Wertheimer, "is a human being, and it is wrong to kill human beings, and that is why you must not destroy the embryo."[2]

Biology

That the fetus is a person is clear from a close examination of biology. From the moment of conception, the fetus is an individual. It is not identical to its father, nor is it identical to its mother. It is a unique child of God, not a carbon copy of anyone else on the planet: "an organism," as a pro-life pharmacist puts it, "unlike any that's ever existed in the past and totally unlike anything that will ever exist again."[3]

This unique personhood, we know today, is present from the beginning. The tiniest fertilized egg is a brand-new life. To kill the fetus, no matter how early in pregnancy, is to destroy this individual person. "Contained within the single cell who I once was," says a right-to-life official, "was the totality of everything I am today."[4] The chromosomes, the genetic codes, the genes—all that will make a child or an adult—are there, ready to be read and acted on like a blueprint, from the first.

Not simply a "potential" human being, as some abortionists claim, the fetus is already human in many, many ways. It moves on its own perhaps as early as the sixth week—well before the mother can feel the movements. It may feel pain at a much earlier stage than previously believed. "Visible under a microscope" after only eight weeks, reports an antiabortion advocate, "are [the fetus's] unique fingerprints, never to change except in size."[5] As for the heart, it has a discernible beat as early as eighteen days after conception. We must not be misled by the fact that the fetus is not immediately recognizable as human, for human it is.

Is a Newborn a Person?

Moreover, the notion that having or lacking "human" traits defines personhood is dangerous and illogical. Consider a newborn. It surely lacks many of the characteristics that we associate with personhood. An eight-day-old baby cannot speak, cannot feed itself, cannot hold its head up, has no teeth. Yet very few people would argue that a mother has the right to kill her eight-day-old. What, then, distinguishes an eight-day-old newborn from a child eight days, weeks, or months after conception?

The answer, shorn of all its rhetoric, is simple: Nothing. The baby is fully human, and so, at each stage of development, is the fetus. Changes are gradual and build on one another. As psychologist Sydney Callahan sums up, "It is hard to defend logically . . . any point after conception as the point at which an immature form of human life is so different from the day before or the day after, that it can be. . . discounted as a nonperson."[6] Thus, there is a seamless, inevitable path connecting the fetus from conception to birth and beyond. This path forces us to accept that human life begins at conception; there is simply no justification to draw an imaginary line elsewhere.

Indeed, as modern science continues to advance, the impossibility of determining any other starting point for life becomes apparent. Concepts such as viability—the fetus's ability to survive outside the womb—are constantly being rethought with newer technology and know-how. Astonishingly small babies who would have died ten or even five years ago can be kept alive today. "This technology," admits feminist thinker Kathleen McDonnell, "is . . . pushing the limits of viability further and further back toward conception."[7] Someday, it will be commonplace for technology to support and nurture the tiniest of fetuses outside the womb. Today, we can save babies born well before their intended due dates, and we can recognize and celebrate their essential humanity. Tomorrow, we will do the same for the smallest fetuses.

That notion has consequences. We do not find it appropriate to dispose of children who are five years or six weeks past birth. When children are viciously killed, we call the act what it is: Murder. We must do the same for children who have yet

Antiabortion activists demonstrate in front of the Supreme Court during the March for Life, an annual pro-life gathering in Washington, D.C.

to be born. As pro-life thinker Stephen Schwarz puts it, "If it is murder at a later stage, it is also murder at an earlier stage. Merely being in another place (the womb), and smaller, cannot take away the reality of murder."[8]

Religion, Culture, and Tradition

That abortion is murder is not merely a matter of biology. Many societies have condemned abortion as murder, with harsh penalties for those who take the fetus's life. The ancient Assyrians, for instance, provided that any woman who killed her fetus "shall be . . . impaled upon a stake and shall not be buried."[9] The recognition that abortion is evil may be rooted in ethical ideas or religious teaching, but the reasoning is always the same: Abortion is murder. Today, many cultures subscribe wholeheartedly to this idea.

The Bible, to name but one example, contains several indictments of abortion. Psalm 139, for instance, includes King David's words: "For Thou didst form my inward parts; Thou didst weave me in my mother's womb. . . . Thine eyes have seen my unformed substance." God breathes life into us at conception ("in my mother's womb"), not at birth. Thus, the Bible recognizes the fetus as fully human. A similar notion is expressed by Jeremiah 1:4: "Before I formed thee in the belly I knew thee, and before thou camest forth out of the womb I sanctified [made holy] thee." God knows us and makes us human while we are still in the womb; He does not wait until our birth to sanctify us or to consider us a full human being worthy of His notice and love. Clearly, God does not define life as beginning with birth.

Guided by these and other biblical passages, Orthodox Jews have traditionally condemned abortion. So, too, have many Christian churches. Early Christian thinkers such as Tertullian and St. Ambrose believed that abortion was murder. As one theologian wrote in the first century A.D., "You shall not kill either the fetus by abortion or the new born." [10] This proscription, based on religious tradition, is still quite strong among Roman Catholics and evangelicals. The Catholic Hospital Association of the United States and Canada states, "Every unborn child must be regarded as a human person, with all the rights of a human person, from the moment of conception." [11] Abortion, according to this long tradition, is murder.

Abortion kills. It destroys a soul, a life—a person. The tradition of many cultures condemns it. Logic shows that it is no different from infanticide, for the fetus is no less human than the newborn. Medical evidence proves the fetus's personhood. The evidence is clear and unmistakable: Abortion is murder.

1. Quoted in "The Pro-Life Advocate." http://members.aol.com/pladvocate.

2. Quoted in Marshall Cohen et al., eds., *The Rights and Wrongs of Abortion*. Princeton, NJ: Princeton University Press, 1974, p. 37.

3. Larry Frieders, "The New Abortionists: Chemical Abortion in Contemporary Culture." www.top.net/vitalsigns/vsmnewabort.html.

4. Quoted in Robert M. Baird and Stuart E. Rosenbaum, *The Ethics of Abortion*. Buffalo: Prometheus Books, 1993, p. 263.

5. "The Pro-Life Advocate."

6. Quoted in Baird and Rosenbaum, *The Ethics of Abortion*, p. 112.

7. Kathleen McDonnell, *Not an Easy Choice*. Toronto: Women's, 1984, p. 45.

8. Stephen Schwarz, "The Moral Question of Abortion," 1990. www.ohiolife.org/mqa/2-3.htm.

9. Quoted in Edward Batchelor Jr., ed., *Abortion: The Moral Issues*. New York: Pilgrim, 1982, p. 186.

10. Quoted in "Historical Abortion Beliefs of the Christian Church." www.religioustolerance.org/abo_hist.htm.

11. Quoted in Batchelor, *Abortion*, p. 65.

"The embryo is not a child. . . . It is not a baby. It is not yet a human being."

Abortion Is Not Murder

Few ideas are as wrongheaded as the notion that abortion is equivalent to murder. Logical, ethical, religious, and medical arguments all demonstrate the inaccuracy of this idea. Morally, legally, and practically, a fetus is not a person. "I have held babies in my hands, and now I held this embryo," reports a Catholic theologian visiting an abortion clinic. "I know the difference."[1]

Biology

Scientific evidence makes it apparent that abortion is not murder. The fetus is at best a *potential* human being and not yet an *actual* human being. The differences between a fetus and a newborn baby are many and profound. Take the sensation of pain. A newborn feels pain; this is apparent by simple observation. Until the very end of pregnancy, however, essentially no evidence exists that a fetus can feel pain. What pro-lifers usually interpret as pain is simply reflex: The synapses are not yet well developed enough to permit the feeling of pain as a true human would experience it.

Other important biological differences exist, too. The cerebrum, the most complex area of the brain, is unformed before the sixth month of gestation, perhaps even later. The lungs do not develop until birth is very near. And, of course, nine out of ten abortions are performed in the first few weeks of pregnancy, when the fetus is still technically an embryo—a two-inch-long piece of "life" that bears no resemblance to a newborn baby at all.

In sum, philosopher Mary Anne Warren concludes, the fetus—even a rather well-advanced one—"is considerably less personlike than is the average mature mammal, indeed the average fish."[2] Few of us speak of the "murder" of fish, and even most of those opposed to the killing of fish recognize the wide gap between the death of a fish and the death of a human child. Why, Warren asks, do we treat the fetus differently?

This question is especially valid because nature is notably hard on fetuses. Pregnancy does not imply delivery—far from it. Perhaps as many as one-third of all fertilized eggs are spontaneously—naturally—aborted. Many of these fertilizations are defective in some way. Others simply do not survive the long gestation period. "It just can't be that every fertilized egg is a human life," says a woman who has had three children. "Too many things go wrong for that."[3] Indeed, it is difficult to call abortion "murder" when nature itself "murders" so many on its own.

Logical Flaws

Logically, in fact, it makes no sense to treat the fetus as life on a par with people already born. It is true, as pro-lifers argue, that there is a continuum from conception to death, a path that leads inevitably from one step to the next. It is a mistake, however, to see this as evidence that the smallest fertilized egg is somehow already a person. Perhaps "life" does begin at conception in some way, but fully human life does not.

Consider an analogy. Is an acorn an oak tree? Not a potential oak tree, not a possible oak tree—an oak tree? The answer, obviously, is no. An oak tree is big, tall, leafy. An acorn is small, curved, smooth. No one could possibly mistake the two for each other. But if an acorn is not an oak tree, then clearly a fertilized egg is not a person either. As writer J.C. Callahan points out, "In the case of the acorn and in the case of the conceptus, at the end of the process, we do have things *very* unlike those at the beginning of the process."[4]

There are other analogies. A blueprint is not a house. A hen's egg is not a chicken. "Few of us are confused about the entity we are eating when we have eggs for breakfast," writes an ethicist. "An egg—even a fertilized egg—is still an egg and not a chicken."[5] Indeed, we run into serious ethical questions when we try to argue that zygotes are people. "Taking this genetic code argument to its extreme," says a writer, "each [cell in the zygote] is encoded with a specific DNA. If each of these cells is then to be considered a possible human being, then any time any cell is removed, through surgery for instance, a potential life is destroyed."[6]

With advances in medical technology, this argument is not just theoretical. Consider the problem raised by the new science of cloning. Scientists will soon be able to grow any cell into a human clone. With cloning, therefore, every cell is potential life—just like a fetus. Could a person be arrested for having cancer cells surgically removed? They are no less "human life" than a newly fertilized egg. And human cells are killed off every day by minor scrapes, cuts, and bruises. "If we say any cell has the potential to be a human being," asks a scientist, "then every time you cut your finger, do you have to wear black?"[7] Clearly, it is ludicrous to think of these potential lives as on a par with actual life. The same is true when dealing with the small clusters of cells that make up a potential human child.

The Real Tradition

Pro-lifers who consider abortion to be murder like to cite tradition to demonstrate their case. But tradition supports the notion that abortion is not murder. Pro-lifers leave out the mass of traditions that have supported and accepted abortion under many—or indeed all—circumstances. The ancient Romans, for example, did not view abortion as murder. The great philosopher Aristotle saw very little wrong with abortion. Plato recommended that women over forty be required to undergo abortions. In fact, few cultures in world history have considered abortion to be murder. Social historian Linda Gordon has written that "almost all preindustrial societies practiced abortion."[8]

Not only do antiabortion forces leave out many cultures when they make their claims, they also stretch and distort the evidence from the traditions that they do cite. Pro-lifers are especially fond of quoting the Bible, for instance, but biblical evidence is far from compelling. The Bible never refers directly to abortion, and it certainly does not forbid it. If anything, the Bible suggests that abortion is not at all the same thing as murder. In Exodus 21, for example, the death penalty is given as the proper punishment for a man who strikes and kills a woman, but a fine is the appropriate sentence if he strikes a pregnant woman who miscarries as a result of the blow. It is hard to see how such a comparatively light penalty could be consistent with the idea that abortion is "killing" a fetus.

Jews and Christians

Nor is it accurate to say that all religious groups in America automatically call abortion murder. Many mainstream American religions today, even those that officially disapprove of abortion, do not view it in the same light as murder. Both Reform and Conservative Judaism, for example, do not. Perhaps using the passage from Exodus as a guide, the twelfth-century Jewish scholar Rashi wrote definitively that the fetus "is not a person."[9] The Talmud, too, indicates that the soul is not present until the time of birth: "The fetus," it says, "is as the thigh of its mother"[10]—only a part of her body. While calling abortion a difficult choice and cautioning that it not be exercised on a whim, most American Jewish leaders agree that abortion cannot be considered murder.

The Christian experience is similar. Many liberal denominations have come to support abortion rights, arguing that abortion is not murder; no church, however, has favored infanticide. Nor has conservative Christianity always believed that life begins at conception. From the fifth century until 1869, the rule of thumb in Catholicism was that male fetuses were not human until forty days after conception; female fetuses, eighty days. Thus, abortion before this period was not murder at all and was not proscribed.

That this attitude still has adherents, even in the more conservative churches, is clear. As one writer points out, "At no time in the history of the [Catholic] Church have an embryo or pre-viable fetus been considered full persons to the extent of being worthy of an individual burial service."[11] In recent years some radical pro-life activists have scheduled mass funerals for aborted fetuses, but this practice is extremely new. Traditionally, all mainstream religions have drawn a distinction between fetuses and full-fledged persons.

So, too, has the legal system of the United States. For most of American history since English settlement began, abortion was legal as long as it was performed before "quickening"—the point at which the mother can detect fetal movement. Even when abortion was made illegal altogether in many areas, the law did not treat abortion as murder. In Texas, for example, "murder" was defined as killing a person who was already born, and the statute governing abortion called for a much less serious penalty.

In fact, as a general rule, the laws of the United States do not recognize the fetus as a "person." Instead, personhood is conferred only on those born alive. Most laws draw a clear and important distinction between already-born people and as-yet-unborn fetuses. If a fetus is not a person, then it cannot be murdered. Whether we examine American laws, Jewish custom, or the traditions of many cultures—including even the Catholic viewpoint over time—it is clear that tradition is squarely on the side of those who argue that abortion cannot be murder.

Abortion is a serious matter. The fetus is a potential life, and its destruction should not be chosen arbitrarily. But there is a major difference between a potential life and a full person, between a bundle of cells and a newborn baby. Tradition and biology agree that abortion cannot be called murder. "The embryo is not a child," sums up pro-choice activist Charles A. Gardner. "It is not a baby. It is not yet a human being."[12]

1. Quoted in Robert M. Baird and Stuart E. Rosenbaum, *The Ethics of Abortion*. Buffalo: Prometheus Books, 1993, p. 146.

2. Quoted in Baird and Rosenbaum, *The Ethics of Abortion*, p. 231.

3. Quoted in Gregg Easterbrook, "Medical Evolution: Will Homo Sapiens Become Obsolete?" *New Republic*, March 1, 1999.

4. Quoted in Baird and Rosenbaum, *The Ethics of Abortion*, p. 253.

5. Quoted in Edward Batchelor Jr., ed., *Abortion: The Moral Issues*. New York: Pilgrim, 1982, p. 183

6. Marlena Sobel, "Abortion Myths," July 1994. www.berkshire.net/~ifas/fw/9407/myths.html.

7. Quoted in Easterbrook, "Medical Evolution."

8. Quoted in Kathleen McDonnell, *Not an Easy Choice*. Toronto: Women's, 1984, p. 42.

9. Quoted in "Past and Present Beliefs of the Christian Church." www.religioustolerance.org/abo_hist.htm.

10. Quoted in Raymond A. Zwerin and Richard J. Shapiro, "Judaism and Abortion," 1996. www.rcrc.org/religion/es/comp.html.

11. "Past and Present Beliefs of the Christian Church."

12. Quoted in Baird and Rosenbaum, *The Ethics of Abortion*, p. 267.

CHAPTER 2

Should Abortion Be Legal?

"[For a woman] to be forced to give birth to a child, against her will, is an overwhelming violation of her freedom."

Abortion Should Be Legal

Should abortion be legal? The answer to that question depends on the values and goals of a society. If a society is in favor of unhealthy and unwanted children, governmental interference in private decisions, and putting women's lives at risk for ideology, then that society should ban abortion. But if a society believes in open dialogue, freedom to make personal decisions, and outstanding health care for every woman and child, then abortion must remain legal. As one pro-choice official puts it, *Roe v. Wade* "has obviously saved enormous numbers of lives, improved women's health, [and] made for stronger families."[1]

No Way to Stop It

Abortion is a fact. It has always been a fact. Since the earliest times women have known of methods to terminate a pregnancy. Even in societies in which abortion is illegal, women who know that bearing a child is not an option have sought out ways to abort. Before *Roe v. Wade* extended abortion rights to all American women during the first trimester of pregnancy, literally thousands of illegal abortions were performed every year across the nation. "It is a great mistake," writes commentator Anna Quindlen, "to believe that if abortion is illegal, it will be non-existent."[2]

Unfortunately, illegal abortion was an extremely dangerous procedure. Too often illegal "clinics" were run by people with no medical training and little or no concern for the health of the women they treated. Horror stories abounded: abortions performed on kitchen tables or in cars, women infected by unsterile tools, women killed by bungling, uncaring abortionists. The fate of a Brooklyn woman in 1963 was all too common. As a reporter described the case, "Someone attempting an amateur abortion had killed her by injecting a caustic solution into her womb."[3]

These stories and figures indicate that making abortion illegal does not keep women from aborting; it simply makes abortion more hazardous. To criminalize abortion will not save babies, even if we wished to argue that two-month-old fetuses can be considered babies. A Catholic priest sums up the problem succinctly: "If *Roe v. Wade* is undone," he says, "there will still be the same number of women who get abortions. The difference will be that women again will be dying."[4] Given such realities, criminalizing abortion simply means sending women back to the unregulated butchers. It is surely better to legalize and to regulate.

Wanted Children

Few people suggest that abortion ought to be chosen without so much as a second thought. And indeed, few women do get an abortion simply because they "feel like it." No woman gets an abortion seven months into pregnancy because she is unable to dance, realizes that her due date will conflict with a concert she would like to attend, or dislikes the way she looks in maternity clothes. Nor do American women typically use abortion in place of other forms of birth control. As obstetrician Don Sloan puts it, "In our almost quarter-century of legalized abortion there are no signs that [substituting abortion for birth control] is a factor."[5] Rather, women have good, thoughtful reasons for choosing abortions, reasons that deserve the protection of the law rather than its disapproval.

Consider one woman's response when asked if she aborted for "mere convenience." "Absolutely ridiculous!" she exploded. "I was already supporting five kids! You're out of your bloody mind! I was working full time and going to school. . . . I slept four hours a night, sometimes three."[6] Reasons to terminate pregnancy vary from woman to woman. Always, however, they are significant reasons—important and legitimate. "That we cannot cope with another child," writes Kathleen McDonnell, "that we are not ready for parenthood, that we cannot face raising a child without a partner, that we cannot afford a child, that our method of birth control failed . . . these are the reasons why we seek abortion in the vast majority of cases."[7]

The truth is, not every pregnant woman is able to adequately care for her child. Some women are in poor health and in no shape to manage an active baby. Others suffer from psychological problems that make caring for children unrealistic. Still others lack the emotional or financial resources to do right by the new arrival. If society forces these women to give birth, their lives may be irretrievably ruined.

So, too, may the child's. Pro-life legislators would force women to bear children, but often the very same people are constantly trying to cut funding from social programs, thus providing no services for the children. And unwanted children need services more than most others. According to one study, 41 percent of women denied abortions were sorry that they had given birth, and fully a third of those surveyed "harbored anger and resentment against these unwanted children."[8] Other studies suggest that unwanted children are more likely to be emotionally unstable, in trouble with the law, and involved in drug abuse. Indeed, the consequences of forcing women to give birth will be unpleasant for everyone involved: mother, child, and all of society. Safe, legal abortion can ensure that every child born is a wanted child.

A Human Rights Issue

Perhaps the most basic reason for keeping abortion legal, however, is that abortion is a human and civil rights issue. A woman required to bear a child she does not want is essentially being held prisoner by the government. Her womb is no longer hers but community property, her body held in hostage to the fetus or embryo within. In an advanced society such as ours, this situation is an abomination. A woman must have the right to make decisions that affect her own body.

This right is most apparent in a few cases, situations in which pregnancy impacts the woman's health or indeed threatens her life. However, the principle extends to any abortion. No person is as affected by a pregnancy as the pregnant woman herself. She alone must have the final say in the decision to abort. As author Roger L. Shinn sums up the argument, for a woman "to be forced to give birth to a child, against her will, is an overwhelming violation of her freedom."[9]

It is easy to see the truth of this by using an analogy. In the words of ethicist Judith Jarvis Thomson, suppose that

> You wake up in the morning and find yourself back to back in bed with an unconscious violinist. A famous unconscious violinist. He has been found to have a fatal kidney ailment, and the Society of Music Lovers has . . . found that you alone have the right blood type to help. They have therefore kidnapped you, and last night the violinist's circulatory system was plugged into yours, so that your kidneys can be used to extract poisons from his blood as well as your own. . . . To unplug you would be to kill him. But . . . it's only for nine months.[10]

Would you be justified in unhooking yourself, even at the loss of the violinist's life? Most people, Thomson believes, would answer yes: The violinist has no claim on you. You may choose to allow the violinist to make use of your body, but he has no automatic right to it.

Neither, by analogy, does the fetus have an unlimited claim on its host. If the woman chooses not to allow the fetus to grow and flourish, then so be it. Just as society must not require people to give over their bodies in service of an unconscious violinist, society may also not make its citizens carry unwanted fetuses for nine months. This right is basic and absolutely essential. "If you can't determine the fate of your body," warns Planned Parenthood's Gloria Feldt, "all other rights pale."[11] To criminalize abortion is to ignore this important right and throw all supposed "rights" into jeopardy.

Women's Rights

Finally, abortion must remain legal in order to provide a level playing field for women and men. Women bear the biggest share of the burden where young children are concerned—not merely because they bear children but also because they alone can provide breast milk and because women traditionally have been given primary responsibility for child care. For a woman to give birth, then, can be a severe handicap in the workplace. "Pregnant women are still expected to quit high-visibility jobs such as waitressing," points out Kathleen McDonnell, "as soon as their pregnancy becomes obvious."[12] Few

Reasoning that abortion will continue to occur even if outlawed, activists contend that a better solution is to keep abortion legal and regulated through licensed clinics. Here, demonstrators attempt to keep a clinic in operation despite the growing hostilities at such centers.

women who take maternity leaves are paid full wages for the time they missed; many find their jobs are not held open for them, or discover that they have been shunted to a less-demanding and lower-status "mommy track."

Men, of course, are rarely treated that way. Men who start families may worry about how to feed and clothe their children, but their employers do not fire them simply for daring to bring babies into the world. Neither do they force male workers to take unwanted or unneeded time off nor demote them to jobs deemed suitable for employees more interested in raising their children than in taking on interesting and exciting projects at work.

Thus, the right to an abortion is basic. A woman who does not want to fall victim to discrimination and patronizing assumptions about her wishes and desires must have the ability to end her pregnancy. The fact that abortion is legal, says one commentator, has "given women the practical wherewithal to pursue their dreams and aspirations without fear of pregnancy shattering those dreams."[13] The gains that women have made over the last generation will all be lost if abortion is made illegal again.

1. Quoted in Jenny Hontz, "Twenty-Five Years Later: The Impact of *Roe v. Wade*," *Human Rights*, Spring 1998, p. 11.

2. Quoted in Robert M. Baird and Stuart E. Rosenbaum, *The Ethics of Abortion*. Buffalo: Prometheus Books, 1993, p. 29.

3. Quoted in Celeste Michelle Condit, *Decoding Abortion Rhetoric*. Urbana: University of Illinois Press, 1990, p. 24.

4. Quoted in Reproductive Health and Rights Center, "U.S. Premiere of Spanish Version of Fadiman Documentary." www.choice.org/12.summaries.html.

5. Quoted in Bonnie Szumski, ed., *Abortion: Opposing Viewpoints*. San Diego: Greenhaven, 1986, p. 46.

6. Quoted in Condit, *Decoding Abortion Rhetoric*, p. 175.

7. Kathleen McDonnell, *Not an Easy Choice*. Toronto: Women's, 1984, p. 55.

8. Alison Landes et al., eds. *Abortion: An Eternal Social and Moral Issue*. Wylie, TX: Information Plus, 1996, p. 123.

9. Quoted in Edward Batchelor Jr., ed., *Abortion: The Moral Issues.* New York: Pilgrim, 1982, p. 168.

10. Quoted in Marshall Cohen et al., eds., *The Rights and Wrongs of Abortion.* Princeton, NJ: Princeton University Press, 1974, pp. 4–5.

11. Quoted in Hontz, "Twenty-Five Years Later," p. 8.

12. McDonnell, *Not an Easy Choice*, p. 73.

13. Quoted in Hontz, "Twenty-Five Years Later," p. 11.

"It should not be illegal to destroy a fetus whose chances for survival are slim or one whose life will be filled with pain and suffering."

Abortion Should Only Be Legal in Certain Cases

Abortion is the taking of a human life, and as such it ought not to be encouraged. Adoption is a better alternative for women who believe they cannot support or manage a child. There are other good alternatives, too: strengthening families, providing support networks, and the like. That said, however, there are a few—a very few—cases in which abortion is justified and ought to be legal. Hard-and-fast rules and blanket prohibitions are rarely as sensible as taking the time to consider all of the ramifications of a situation.

Precedent

The idea that some exceptions are necessary is not new. Long before abortion was widely permitted, forward-thinking state legislatures permitted abortion in a few unusual cases. The American Law Institute's 1959 model statute allowed abortion in only three cases:

1. If continuation of the pregnancy "would gravely impair the physical or mental health of the mother";

2. If the doctor believed "that the child would be born with grave physical or mental defects," or

3. If the pregnancy resulted from rape or incest.[1]

Many states, among them Maryland, Kansas, and New Mexico, adopted these guidelines, often with little or no debate. Although most of these legislatures were solidly pro-life, individual legislators recognized that permitting abortion in these three situations was not at all the same as voting for abortion on demand. Indeed, other pro-life nations have followed suit: Guatemala and El Salvador are two examples of largely Catholic countries in which some or all of these laws are in place.

Not only are these exceptions codified in law, they have a strong moral history as well. The Lutheran Church, Missouri Synod, for example, rarely allows abortion but does make an exception to "prevent the birth of a severely crippled, deformed or abnormal infant."[2] In Jewish law, report two experts, "even the most stringent of authorities permit an abortion to save the life of a pregnant woman."[3] And the Southern Baptist Church is one of many that sees a justification for permitting abortion in cases of rape and incest, without giving women a blank check to have abortions whenever and for whatever reason they wish.

It should be stressed, moreover, that these three exceptions make up only a tiny percentage of all abortions. Former U.S. surgeon general C. Everett Koop, a physician, has said that he never once saw a case in which abortion was necessary to save a woman's life. According to a 1988 study in the journal *Family Planning Perspectives*, only three of every hundred abortions is performed primarily because of worries about birth defects; rape and incest victims together account for only 1 percent of all U.S. abortions. To permit abortion in these few restricted cases is hardly the same as starting down a slippery slope in which abortion on demand becomes the logical next step.

Rape and Incest

Perhaps the most obvious of these cases would be ones in which the fetus was created as a result of a sexual crime—rape or incest. It is certainly true that the fetus created in this way is innocent of any wrongdoing. Yet so is the woman who would otherwise be forced to bear her attacker's child. She did not consent to sex, did not have the choice to use birth control; she should be given the choice whether to have the baby. The alternative is uncivilized and cruel. We believe in loving parents for every child, yet how is a woman to love her child when its very existence brings back terrible memories? This is perhaps even more true where incest is concerned. To tell a twelve-year-old child who is impregnated by her stepfather that she must have the baby violates her a second time.

Most philosophers, even pro-life ones, recognize this fact. Susan Nicholson argues that there is a moral distinction between women who purposely had sexual intercourse, knowing it could make them pregnant, and women who were not seeking sex. Any woman has "a parental duty to administer to the needs of a human being conceived through her voluntary intercourse," she writes, rejecting the notion of abortion on demand for most women. "The raped woman, on the other hand, does not voluntarily participate in the act producing a new human being. Consequently, she has no parental duty prior to the child's birth."[4] That fact justifies her in having an abortion, if she so chooses.

It is also important that society not try to read God's mind concerning rape and incest. True, no one can know what God has in mind for children born of rape and incest. As one writer cautions, "Good can come from evil,"[5] and there may be a greater purpose than we suspect. But rape and incest are horrible crimes that damage real people's lives. It seems unlikely that a kind and loving God would wish a rape victim to go through with a pregnancy. "If it is a terrible thing to play God by terminating physical life," an ethicist warns, "it is also a terrible thing, in another sense, to play God by imposing as a di-

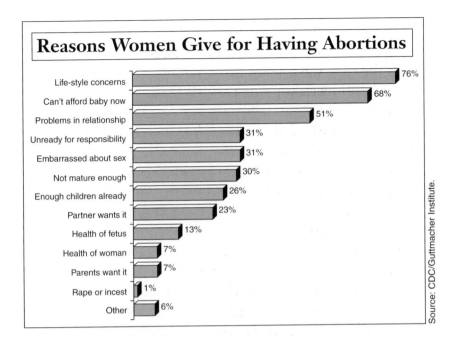

Reasons Women Give for Having Abortions

Reason	Percentage
Life-style concerns	76%
Can't afford baby now	68%
Problems in relationship	51%
Unready for responsibility	31%
Embarrassed about sex	31%
Not mature enough	30%
Enough children already	26%
Partner wants it	23%
Health of fetus	13%
Health of woman	7%
Parents want it	7%
Rape or incest	1%
Other	6%

Source: CDC/Guttmacher Institute.

vine absolute a prohibition that may cause immense suffering both to individuals and society."[6]

Certainly a woman who wishes to keep her baby, even the baby of her rapist, ought to be allowed and encouraged to do so, but it is dangerous to assume that her perspective is the normal one—or should be. "Because of my circumstances," writes a pro-life woman who was raped and impregnated by her brother-in-law, "[abortion] was better for both the embryo and me."[7] Many women will have such a reaction. Rape and incest are reasonable exceptions to illegal abortion.

Birth Defects

A pregnancy in which the baby suffers from a congenital birth defect is just as tragic as a pregnancy caused by rape or incest. These pregnancies are for the most part wanted, sometimes desperately so. Yet the prospects for such children are bleak. They are condemned to live out short lives in pain or virtual unconsciousness; or their lives are long and hard and place unfair burdens on their parents and society.

Years ago nature would have taken many of these children before birth or shortly afterward. Today, modern medicine can do wonders in extending their lives. It may well not be worth the effort, however. New techniques such as amniocentesis can give us information on potential birth defects even when the child is still in the womb. When the results are positive, abortion is often the result. Again, it would be a mistake to condemn all parents who go through with abortion when they learn of these congenital defects.

The reality is that some babies face life with half a brain, with bone malformations, or with their senses permanently impaired. "Every person deserves a fair chance at a good life, and this child wouldn't have that chance," writes one woman explaining her decision to abort a fetus with an extra chromosome. "He would . . . be an outcast, the object of stares and pity, perhaps even ridicule."[8] The quality of life for children such as these is low or nonexistent.

The lack of support systems and the effect on parents is another compelling reason for keeping abortion legal in the case of birth defects. "The realities of raising a child who would never grow to independence would call forth more than we could muster," reports another woman who chose abortion. "The health care, schools, [and necessary] therapies . . . are inadequately available, and horrendously expensive in America."[9] Nor is it clear that the result is worth the struggle.

Of course, just as with rape and incest, some women choose to keep their babies despite the birth defects they will carry. They deserve commendation and respect for making such a hard choice. But it should not be illegal to destroy a fetus whose chances for survival are slim or one whose life will be filled with pain and suffering. The women who choose abortion for these reasons undergo much pain in the process, but they are motivated by the best of reasons: by the love of their children and the desire not to cause them excessive suffering. For these women, their fetuses, and all of society, we must keep abortion legal in these few cases.

1. Quoted in Colin Francome, *Abortion Freedom: A Worldwide Movement.* London: George Allen and Unwin, 1984, p. 102.

2. Quoted in Thomas W. Hilgers et al., *New Perspectives on Human Abortion.* Frederick, MD: Aletheia Books, 1981, p. 401.

3. Raymond A. Zwerin and Richard J. Shapiro, "Judaism and Abortion," 1996. www.rcrc.org/religion/es/comp.html.

4. Quoted in Hilgers, *New Perspectives on Human Abortion,* p. 430.

5. David C. Reardon, "Rape, Incest, and Abortion: Searching Beyond the Myths." www.prolife.org/afterabortion/rape.html.

6. Quoted in Edward Batchelor Jr., ed., *Abortion: The Moral Issues.* New York: Pilgrim, 1982, p. 109.

7. Quoted in Tamara L. Roleff, ed., *Abortion: Opposing Viewpoints.* San Diego: Greenhaven, 1997, p. 133.

8. Quoted in Bonnie Szumski, ed., *Abortion: Opposing Viewpoints.* San Diego: Greenhaven, 1986, p. 112.

9. Quoted in Szumski, *Abortion,* p. 111.

"Since Roe v. Wade *became law, the number of abortions
in America has more than doubled. . . . Legalized abortion
has desensitized Americans to the horrors and the violence of
the act."*

Abortion Should
Be Illegal

Legal abortion is a sham and a disgrace. Far from liberating
women and safeguarding civil rights, abortion leads directly to
a disregard for human life and to the establishment of a culture of violence and irresponsibility. No matter what proabortion thinkers may say, abortion has never solved any
woman's problems. Moreover, abortion pits women against
their children by completely ignoring the very real rights of
the fetus. Legal abortion must not be allowed to continue.

Abortion Myths

Many myths are disseminated by the proabortion community.
Abortion, we are told by pro-choice activists, is impossible to
eliminate. If abortion is made illegal, then illegal clinics will
spring up all over, many with unsanitary facilities and poor
treatment; women, we are told, will die.

But this theory makes little sense. Murder is all too common across the United States. Murder is illegal, but nothing
our society has tried has succeeded in eliminating it. Shall we
simply make murder legal? Of course, no one—not even the
staunchest supporter of a woman's "right" to choose death for

her baby—makes this argument. We do not usually legalize unwanted behavior so that we can avoid policing it. Thus, the argument that abortions will be performed anyway fails on the basis of analogy.

Nor is this argument convincing on its own merits. It is clear that the availability of legal abortion encourages women to abort. Under *Roe v. Wade*, abortion is legal, advertised, in some cases recommended. The Yellow Pages list clinics; names of abortion providers are passed around openly. Today, it is not necessary for a woman to break the law and be forced into a shady underground to have an abortion. If lawbreaking were required, then surely many women would have second thoughts. Who wants to go to jail or pay a heavy fine?

Moreover, by allowing abortion, the government has lost the ability to take a moral stand. Criminalizing abortion would send a clear ethical message to millions of pregnant women: that this society does not include abortion among appropriate responses to unwanted pregnancy. Legal abortion creates an abortion culture in which the procedure has the official stamp of approval from society. Abolish abortion, though, and abortion must go underground. Hospitals would once again be places for the sick, clinics could no longer publish their toll-free numbers, and abortion would be, most appropriately, out of sight. Again, the moral force inherent in outlawing abortion would certainly cause many women to have second thoughts on the subject.

Either way, the result of making abortions illegal would be fewer abortions every year, as some women decided to follow the law or to accept society's moral judgment. How many? Perhaps hundreds of thousands. Perhaps, especially at first, the numbers might be lower, but no one could doubt that making abortion illegal would save at least a few fetuses from an early death. And to a right-to-lifer, any baby saved is a reason to rejoice. Because of pro-lifers who encouraged women to change their minds about having abortions, writes an activist, hundreds of children "who would otherwise have been disposed of in a medical garbage can, are *alive today*."[1]

Another myth is that abortion is now a safe procedure for a woman. It is not. It is far from safe. "Abortion is a surgical procedure," points out pro-lifer Carolyn Gargaro. "It still puts many women at risk."[2] Women have been maimed and paralyzed in "safe," legal abortions. A blood infection resulting from a poorly performed abortion killed an eighteen-year-old in Alabama; a forty-three-year-old Californian, the mother of five, bled to death. Another California woman's uterus was perforated during surgery. She did not survive. "Who needs back alleys," asks a commentator, "when you can get the same gore in a Main Street 'reproductive health center'?"[3] It is not at all clear that illegal abortions would endanger women's lives any more than legal abortions.

"Wanted" Children

Similarly, abortion advocates are fond of saying that abortion reduces child suffering by assuring that all children are "wanted." In fact, abortion has done nothing at all to guarantee wanted babies. Child abuse rates have soared since the legalization of abortion: from about 675,000 reported cases across America in 1976 to 3 million in 1994. Despite easy access to abortion, society today is not rid of incompetent parents, impoverished families, and single-parent households, as the proabortion forces argued it would be.

Worse, permitting abortion encourages the rise of a culture of violence. What is abortion but a violent act made even more appalling by being committed by a parent against her own child? Abortion teaches that problems are best solved through violent means. Mother Teresa said it best: "Any country that accepts abortion is not teaching its people to love, but to use . . . violence to get what they want."[4]

Likewise, abortion encourages selfishness and irresponsibility. Why accept the consequences for your actions when an abortion clinic is handy? This attitude seeps into the culture, too, and the result is a heedless, self-centered people more interested in claiming rights than accepting responsibility.

"When we take actions that cheapen the sanctity of life," writes former U.S. representative Robert K. Dornan, "we are contributing to an overall decline in our society's moral values."[5]

There is a deeper philosophical problem with the notion of "wanted" children, too. As one thinker points out, "Should a human being's right to existence depend solely on how much it is desired by another?"[6] The view that "unwanted" children should simply be disposed of has serious implications for the old, the chronically ill, the mentally retarded, and the disabled. Indeed, we are all affected by the logical extensions of this pro-choice argument. "If 'they' can discard unborn children, maybe even handicapped infants and old people, what's to stop them from discarding you or me?"[7] summarizes Kathleen McDonnell.

In fact, virtually every newborn is wanted by someone, even if not by its biological parents. Adoption waiting lists are long. In 1992 approximately 1.5 million Americans were wanting to adopt, a figure that far outweighed the less than 100,000 available babies but only slightly exceeded the number of babies legally aborted that year. Many families would love to share their hearts and lives with a baby, yet abortion deprives them of this opportunity. "Please give me the child [who would otherwise be aborted]," said the great humanitarian Mother Teresa. "I am willing to accept any child who would be aborted."[8] Carry a baby just nine months, a baby of any race, either gender, healthy or not, and there can be a happy ending. Make abortion illegal, and there will be many more of these happy endings.

Social Problems

A woman faced with an unplanned pregnancy need not place the child for adoption, however. Keeping the baby is often a very real alternative. Nearly all abortions are performed for so-called social reasons: the mother is poor, immature, unmarried, or afraid that a baby might change her life for the worse. By one estimate, reasons such as these account for nearly nineteen out of twenty abortions.

To be sure, these are real concerns that certainly do affect a woman's ability to raise a child. Nevertheless, asks one commentator, "under what other circumstances would we accept the idea that one person has the right to kill another person to solve his or her social problems?"[9] Moreover, many of these problems are reparable. Adoption, as mentioned, is a realistic goal for those who truly cannot manage to care for a child.

But there are other, less permanent solutions, too. Pair a young and frightened teenage mother with an older woman of the community. Make sure that poor, unskilled women get the training they need to get and keep better jobs. Deputize church members to provide emotional support and part-time child care for women abandoned by their partners. The possibilities are endless. "[Society's] mistake," writes Frederica Mathewes-Green, the former vice president of Feminists for Life of America, "was in . . . deciding that the fault lay with the woman, that she should be the one to change. We focused on her swelling belly, not the pressures that made her so desperate."[10]

"They're Forgetting Someone"

The central pro-choice myth, however, is that a woman's pregnancy is only the business of the woman herself. The proabortion lobby likes to couch debate in terms of a woman's right to choose, a woman's right to her body, and so on. But rights are not the sole province of the mother. As a billboard with an ultrasound photo of a fetus declares, "Stop Abortion: They're Forgetting Someone."[11]

Naturally, a woman has a right to her own body. If she develops a wart, a tumor, or a sixth finger and wishes to have these removed, then she should do so. But abortion is different. "It is not [the woman's] body, after all, that is being murdered," says a professor, "it is someone else's."[12] A fetus is not a wart, a tumor, or a sixth finger. Warts, tumors, and fingers do not have humanity themselves; they cannot grow and develop into adults. A fetus does; it can and it will.

As strong as a woman's right to her body may be, then, this right cannot be stronger than the fetus's right to life. "Being a woman myself," writes Carolyn Gargaro, "I am obviously against people trying to control women or their bodies. But the fetus is a completely separate life from the mother. . . . It is not just part of the mother's body."[13] Being asked to carry a baby to term may represent a hardship and may even put a stress on the woman, but the alternative is to completely destroy another life. The two are not comparable in their effects.

Nor is abortion justifiable on the shaky premise of property rights—that women's bodies are their property, and they are entitled to do whatever they wish with them. Even some pro-choice thinkers see that this argument fails to stand up to scrutiny. As one writes, "Mere ownership does not give me the right to kill innocent people whom I find on my property. . . . It is equally unclear that I have any moral right to expel an innocent person from my property when I know that doing so will result in his death."[14] Fairness demands that the fetus's right to life be taken into account. Indeed, fairness requires that this right supersede the woman's right to her body.

No Exceptions

What, then, of the hard cases? What of sexual violence—of the children created by rape and by incest? What of the children burdened with defects that will most likely cause them to die soon after birth or live as near-vegetables? In all cases, the answer is clear. Abortion must still be illegal. A life is a life, no matter what. Rape and incest are terrible crimes, but the babies that grow as a result of them are innocent. As professor Michael Bauman writes, "A child does not lose its right to life simply because its father or mother was a sexual criminal or a deviate."[15] The baby is not responsible for its father's misdeeds. It should not pay for them with its life. Yet, in a cruel twist of irony, while the father cannot be put to death for his crime, his child can.

Furthermore, although public opinion is not always a reliable guide for making moral and legal choices, a study of pregnant rape victims run by Dr. Sandra Mahkorn showed that at least three-quarters of the subjects decided not to have abortions. Young incest victims pressed to have abortions often regret having undergone the procedure. For those who avoided abortion, life is what counts. "All children are gifts from God," says a woman who gave birth to a daughter conceived by rape. "It makes no difference how they are conceived."[16]

Birth Defects

Likewise, abortion must not be made legal in cases of birth defects. Medical science is steadily improving, and a condition that is debilitating today may not be so tomorrow. Besides, it is dangerous to assume that no life is better than a life of low quality. "My life of disability has not been easy or carefree," writes a woman suffering from a neuromuscular condition. Still, she adds, "If I were asked for an opinion on whether to bring a child into the world, knowing she would have the same limitations and opportunities I have had, I would not hesitate to say, 'Yes.'"[17] The term *quality of life*, clearly, is subject to the same issues as the term *wanted child*.

Allowing abortion for birth defects presents further issues. Who is to say that a particular condition is severe enough to warrant abortion? These days, abortion is not used as a "cure" only for seriously damaging conditions such as spina bifida and Tay-Sachs disease. It is increasingly common for babies with much less significant impairments, such as Down's syndrome, to be aborted as well. But it is difficult to consider Down's syndrome in the same league as the more debilitating issues. "Most Down's [syndrome] children, with love and care," argues one commentator, "can lead happy, productive, surprisingly independent lives."[18] Indeed, most Down's syndrome children are relatively healthy.

And allowing abortions for the "health" and "quality of life" of the baby is a slippery slope, especially if all children are to be so-called wanted children. Already, in some nations, carrying a female fetus is seen as a reason to terminate the pregnancy. Today, Down's syndrome is widely considered acceptable as a reason within the medical community. Tomorrow, will it be short stature? Left-handedness? Nearsightedness? In one recent poll cited by philosopher Dianne N. Irving, "close to 30% of the respondents replied that they would abort their child if they knew in advance it would be obese."[19] With early genetic screening more and more possible, aborting children with a predisposition toward obesity is not simply theoretical.

Indeed, from permitting abortions for Down's syndrome, it is a short step to the logical conclusion: *anything* parents do not want becomes a handicapping condition justifying abortion. Parents who discover that their child has the genes for blue eyes rather than brown may wantonly destroy her before she has a chance to take her first breath. Parents who have set their hearts on a tall, blond, right-handed boy need not accept anything less than perfection; all they must do is abort, and conceive again. If this sounds reminiscent of Adolf Hitler's attempt to build a "master race," it should. Permit abortion in one circumstance, and suddenly a whole variety of abortions are justified.

Finally, allowing abortion based on genetic abnormalities presents another issue: those less-than-perfect fetuses who somehow evade genetic testing and are actually born. If it is all right to murder them in the third or sixth month of gestation, why may they not be murdered upon birth? Yet few people would argue that a Down's syndrome newborn should be killed. Similarly, most would not argue that a young adult who acquires a chronic illness would be better off dead; why, then, would anyone assume that the circumstances are different for a preterm baby? Allowing these exceptions to illegal abortion opens the door to a whole new set of equally valid reasons why certain less-than-perfect children and adults ought to be destroyed.

Sadly, we are already on this slippery slope. One exception has led to another. The unhappy result is that since *Roe v.*

Wade became law, the number of abortions in America has more than doubled, and the abortion rate has climbed, too. More and more, abortion is seen as a matter of convenience, not a matter of life and death. Legalized abortion has desensitized Americans to the horrors and the violence of the act. Failing to draw a firm line anywhere has led to this sorry state of affairs. As pro-lifer Nellie Gray observed in 1978, "Once you tolerate a little bit of abortion the abortionist steps in and walks right through the law."[20]

At heart, abortion is about killing innocent victims. How the victim was conceived, how healthy it may be, or whether it is "wanted"—all that does not matter. For the sake of the victims, at the very least, abortion must stop, and among the first steps toward that end is to make it illegal. After all, there can be no legal compromise with murder.

1. Quoted in Robert M. Baird and Stuart E. Rosenbaum, *The Ethics of Abortion.* Buffalo: Prometheus Books, 1993, p. 138.

2. Carolyn Gargaro, "My Views as a Pro-Life Woman." www.gargaro.com/abortion.html.

3. Quoted in Pro-Life America, "Women Killed by Abortion." www.prolife.com/DEADWMN.html.

4. Quoted in Tamara L. Roleff, ed., *Abortion: Opposing Viewpoints.* San Diego: Greenhaven, 1997, p. 50.

5. Quoted in Alison Landes et al., eds., *Abortion: An Eternal Social and Moral Issue.* Wylie, TX: Information Plus, 1996, p. 203.

6. Candace C. Crandall, "The Fetus Beat Us," *Women's Quarterly,* Winter 1996.

7. Kathleen McDonnell, *Not an Easy Choice.* Toronto: Women's, 1984, p. 92.

8. Quoted in Roleff, *Abortion,* p. 51.

9. "Why Women Have Abortions." www.infinet.com/~life/stats/whyabort.htm.

10. "*Roe v. Wade*—Twenty-Five Years of Life Denied." www.roevwade.org/women.html.

11. Quoted in Celeste Michelle Condit, *Decoding Abortion Rhetoric.* Urbana: University of Illinois Press, 1990, p. 84.

12. Michael Bauman, "Verbal Plunder: Combating the Feminist Encroachment on the Language of Theology and Ethics," 1996. www.christiananswers.net/summit/plunder.html.

13. Gargaro, "My Views as a Pro-Life Woman."

14. Quoted in "Abortion Fact Sheet," 1995. www.christiananswers.net/summit/abrtfact.html.

15. Bauman, "Verbal Plunder."

16. Quoted in Roleff, *Abortion*, p. 138.

17. Quoted in Roleff, *Abortion*, p. 128.

18. Quoted in Roleff, *Abortion*, p. 125.

19. Dianne N. Irving, "NIH and Human Embryo Research Revisited: What Is Wrong with This Picture?" 1999. www.all.org/abac/dni002.htm.

20. Quoted in Colin Francome, *Abortion Freedom: A Worldwide Movement*. London: George Allen and Unwin, 1984, p. 191.

CHAPTER 3

Should Abortion Rights Be Restricted?

*"Far from being performed only in worst-case scenarios . . .
[partial-birth abortion] is all too often a backup plan for
women too ignorant or self-centered to make a decision earlier
in their pregnancies."*

Partial-Birth Abortions Should Be Banned

Few medical procedures are so grisly—and so unnecessary—as partial-birth abortion. This operation is performed only on late-term fetuses too fully developed for "normal" surgical abortion. It involves the partial delivery of the baby, followed by its brutal killing at the hands of a doctor. A group of Southern Baptist leaders describes the operation:

> With ultrasound for guidance, a doctor uses forceps and hands to deliver an intact baby feet first until only the head remains in the birth canal. The doctor pierces the base of the baby's skull with surgical scissors. He or she then inserts a canula [drainage tube] into the incision and suctions out the brain of the baby so the head can be collapsed.[1]

Such a gruesome procedure has no place in a civilized society. Partial-birth abortion must be banned.

More than a Potential Life

There can be no question that a five-to-seven-month-old fetus (the stage at which partial-birth abortion is most likely to be performed) is much more than a potential human being.

Even many of those who believe in abortion on demand during the first trimester accept this truth. At seven months, most parts of the body are well formed. The fetus looks like a post-birth baby and has many of the attributes of one. Indeed, fetuses of that age have been born prematurely and have survived. On what authority do we determine that some of these children are viable and some are to be disposed of?

In particular, partial-birth abortion creates terrible pain for the well-developed fetus. "Without a doubt, [partial-birth abortion] is a dreadfully painful experience," reports a surgeon who has studied the issue. "The fetus within this time of gestation, 20 weeks and beyond, is fully capable of experiencing pain."[2] There is no hedging, as there is with fetuses in the first few weeks: Preborn children in the final months of pregnancy do feel pain. We have no ethical right to inflict such pain on one who is innocent of any wrongdoing.

Supporters of partial-birth abortion often claim that the anesthesia used in the operation renders the fetus incapable of feeling. That claim is extremely dubious; no less an authority than the American Society of Anesthesiologists argues that "pain relief for the fetus is doubtful"[3] when general anesthetics are given, and that local anesthetics have no effect on the baby whatever.

Nor is there evidence that anesthesia kills the baby outright, as some apologists for partial-birth abortion have argued. Martin Haskell, an Ohio abortionist who pioneered a method of late abortion, admits that most fetuses aborted this way are alive until the end of the procedure, despite anesthesia. It stands to reason, too, that if anesthesia is insufficient to ease pain, it is unlikely to kill. The cold, hard fact is that partial-birth abortion kills the fetus—brutally.

The Numbers

Against such pain and suffering, we must, of course, weigh the need for this procedure. Proponents of partial-birth abortion frequently refer to the process as extremely rare—perhaps five or six hundred cases a year. Indeed, abortion industry groups such as

ANOTHER COVERUP

the National Abortion Federation and Planned Parenthood have consistently argued that partial-birth abortion is performed "only when the woman's life is at risk or the fetus has a condition incompatible with life."[4] If, as these advocates claim, every partial-birth abortion did represent the saving of a mother's life or the removal of a baby who could never be born alive, then it would be hard to argue against partial-birth abortion.

However, the pro-choice forces are seriously mistaken—or, perhaps, lying. The true number of partial-birth abortions is many times the five hundred we are regularly given. How many, no one can tell for sure; as a pro-life advertisement points out, "Clinics are not legally bound to report partial-birth abortions."[5] But the numbers we do know, even ones given privately by pro-choice doctors and organizations, tell a very different story.

Ron Fitzsimmons, executive director of the National Coalition of Abortion Providers, used to toe the party line regarding the number of partial-birth abortions performed; like other pro-choice officials, he estimated that five or six hundred were performed per year. Now? "I lied through my teeth," he admits. "We should tell [the public] the truth."[6] Two pioneering abortionists alone, Martin Haskell and James McMahon, have performed over three thousand partial-birth abortions. A New Jersey clinic reports that it uses the procedure on as many as fifteen hundred women every year. The "official" pro-choice numbers are, frankly, unbelievable.

Maternal Depression and Cleft Palate

The reasons given for late-term abortion are equally preposterous. Surgeons have performed partial-birth abortions for reasons ranging from maternal depression to cleft palate (a disorder of the mouth and upper jaw), hardly the endangerment of life or the fatal deformities to which the pro-choice groups like to point. Partial-birth abortions are "primarily done on healthy women and healthy fetuses,"[7] admits Fitzsimmons. The real reasons for the procedure are much the same as the reasons women give for wanting early abortions, with the exception that the women in question did not know, or perhaps did not care, how far along their pregnancy was.

Unfortunately, the proabortion side has dominated the partial-birth debate. Advocates for the procedure have repeatedly misrepresented it as a rarity, done only after much careful thought and for the most unselfish of reasons. As a result, partial-birth abortion remains a legal reality.

However, there are signs of change. Bills to ban the procedure were sent to President Clinton's desk in both 1996 and 1998; he has vetoed them both times, but the majority of senators and representatives are in favor of eliminating partial-birth abortions. Public opinion polls consistently indicate that Americans are far from comfortable with keeping this form of abortion legal. A 1998 Associated Press survey, for instance, found that 79 percent of Americans wanted to see the procedure forbidden. The American Medical Association has declared that partial-birth abortion "is not good medicine"[8] and has even supported legislation to restrict its use.

As the facts of partial-birth abortion become better known,

we can hope that the procedure will be made illegal. Partial-birth abortion is a cruel and disgusting process morally equivalent to infanticide. Far from being performed only in worst-case scenarios in which no decision can be considered a good one, it is all too often a backup plan for women too ignorant or self-centered to make a decision earlier in their pregnancies. A civilized nation should not permit the procedure. Partial-birth abortion ought to be against the law.

1. Quoted in Baptist Message Online, "SBC Leaders Decry Recent Abortion Veto, Urge Clinton to Repent of Action," June 20, 1996. www.lacollege.edu/baptist/message/6.20.96/6.20.96.abortion.html

2. Quoted in "Partial Birth Abortion: Background Info." www.prolifeinfo.org/pba.html.

3. Quoted in Tamara L. Roleff, ed., *Abortion: Opposing Viewpoints*. San Diego: Greenhaven, 1997, p. 76.

4. Quoted in "Abortion Advocates Lie About Anesthesia." www.roevwade.org/advocates.html.

5. Paid advertisement, *Washington Post National Weekly Edition*, January 18, 1999, p. 2.

6. "Abortion Advocate Admits Deception." www.prolife.org/rvw/ad1.html.

7. Quoted in "Abortion Advocates Lie About Anesthesia."

8. Paid advertisement, *Washington Post National Weekly Edition*, p. 2.

"Abortion opponents are attempting to use the existence of a few unrepresentative [partial-birth] abortions as an excuse to roll back a quarter century of progress in women's rights."

Partial-Birth Abortions Should Not Be Banned

Abortion opponents are not always as careful with their words as they ought to be. Words and phrases like *pro-life*, *family values*, and *babykillers* are misleading or just plain wrong. Perhaps the most blatant example, though, is the term *partial-birth abortion*. There is, quite simply, no such thing. As used by those who oppose abortion rights, the phrase refers vaguely to any of several procedures that can be used in late-term abortions. The most well known of these, thanks to the efforts of the right-to-lifers, is intact dilation and evacuation (known as D&E or—under a slightly different name—D&X), which the public mistakenly calls partial-birth abortion.

Intact D&E is a very serious undertaking. It is an operation that involves suctioning the fetus's brain out of its skull. A major piece of surgery? Of course. An operation to be taken lightly? Of course not. The only type of late-term abortion? Not at all. Intact D&E is, however, the most graphic and unsettling of all of the various procedures used to abort fetuses beyond the first trimester of pregnancy. Small wonder, then, that the forces opposing late-term abortions act as if it were the only possible method. Small wonder—but misleading and wrong.

Limited Use

In fact, the procedure as usually described is extremely rare. There are good reasons for this. It is invasive, and it does indeed create stresses for both the woman and the fetus. "Intact D&E," a pro-choice organization points out, "is used only when other [late-term] procedures, such as induced labor or vaginal delivery, would present higher risk to the woman's life, health, or future childbearing."[1] It is a gruesome procedure; of that there can be no doubt, and other procedures are used for most, indeed nearly all, later abortions.

However, intact D&E is sometimes the most effective choice available. Ideology aside, doctors know that this procedure—like many other "gruesome" surgeries—nevertheless has value. The American College of Obstetricians and Gynecologists (ACOG) has stated that it "may be the best or most appropriate procedure in a particular circumstance to save the life or preserve the health of a woman."[2] Most of the time, it is not the best solution, but it ought to remain legal for the few cases in which it is.

Nor is intact D&E used indiscriminately. Sadly, there is a need for late-term abortions. Severe birth defects do not always manifest themselves early in pregnancy: In the case of Claudia Crown Ades, only a third-trimester ultrasound revealed that her son had severe heart, brain, and organ malformations. Moreover, women's lives and health are put at risk by disasters during pregnancy: ruptured uteruses, internal bleeding, and permanent infertility are all possible problems created by carrying a fetus into the final trimester. Technological know-how cannot solve every fetal defect or medical crisis. Sometimes intact D&E is the most ethical solution to a tragic situation. As syndicated columnist Ellen Goodman puts it, "This procedure is sometimes the best of the rotten options."[3]

When a pregnancy cannot have a happy outcome, partial birth abortion may be indicated.

Finally, it is not up to the public to make the judgment of when late-term abortion may be used. Neither is it up to legislators, however well intentioned they may be. "Only the doctor," ACOG goes on to say, "in consultation with the patient, based upon the woman's particular circumstances, can make this decision."[4] To say otherwise is to allow laymen and ideologues to set medical policy. That, says the dean of the Columbia School of Public Health, is "highly inappropriate"; moreover, it "could have devastating consequences on the quality of medical care in America."[5]

No Good Choices

The case of Tammy Watts is instructive. After seven months of pregnancy, an ultrasound revealed every woman's worst nightmare: major congenital defects. The fetus had six fingers, no eyes, and damaged kidneys; the heart was abnormal; several internal organs were growing outside the body. "Knowing our baby was going to die," said Watts, "and would probably suffer a good deal in doing so, my husband and I made the choice"[6] to have an intact D&E.

On what basis do the antiabortion forces wish to force Watts and others like her to continue two more months with a failed pregnancy? On what basis do they wish to deny late-term abortions to women in mortal danger from unexpected occurrences in pregnancy, like the one whose uterus would likely have ruptured unless the fetus was removed at once? Whose interests are served by removing the possibility of late-term abortion? Watts and her husband were faced with a terrible choice. But it is clear that they did not choose randomly or without consideration of the consequences. For Watts, as for a few hundred other American women in similar situations every year, late-term abortion offers the best, most humane alternative imaginable.

President Bill Clinton sees the issues more clearly than

most. Here, he explains his veto of a bill that would have banned partial-birth abortions:

> I do not support the use of this procedure on demand or on the strength of mild or fraudulent health complaints. But I do believe it is wrong to abandon women . . . whose doctors advise them that they need the procedure to avoid serious injury. That, in my judgment, would be the true inhumanity. . . . Some may believe it is morally superior to compel a woman to endure serious risks to her health . . . in order to deliver a baby who is already dead or about to die. I am not among them.[7]

Serious risks to a woman's health, "a baby who is already dead or about to die"—that is why intact D&E must remain legal, and indeed, that is why the vast majority of these procedures are performed.

Reasons for Late-Term Abortions

Granted, some second-term abortions are performed for reasons that make many people uncomfortable. By no means are all fourth- or fifth-month procedures done because of concerns about birth defects or the mother's health. Since abortion raises more disturbing ethical questions the later it is performed, it is hard to defend the choices of women who waited several months to abort. Elective abortions performed during the fifth or sixth month should give even the most hardened pro-choice advocate pause.

Still, it is not up to us to judge the validity of a woman's wish to terminate her pregnancy. And it is worth considering why a woman, especially a teenager, might not have gotten an abortion earlier on. Did she perhaps not know enough about her body to know that she was pregnant earlier on? Many right-to-lifers oppose sex education in schools. Was she perhaps ignorant of birth control? Many right-to-lifers are uncomfortable promoting birth control, insisting instead on abstinence—an unrealistic goal for many women. Did she wish her pregnancy would merely "go away"? Many pro-lifers avoid overt discussion of sexuality, preferring to keep the subject hidden. Or did she perhaps consider abortion, only to be met at the clinic by protesters carrying signs, blocking the doors, and even threatening violence? The fault may not be the woman's alone.

Banning Most Abortions

Antichoice groups are deliberately vague about the meaning of the term *partial-birth abortion*. The reason is public relations: They want to argue from two sides at once. On the one hand, they want to argue that partial-birth abortion is cruel and violent, so they describe one particularly unpleasant late-term procedure—intact D&E—in their literature and ignore everything else. On the other hand, they want to argue that partial-birth abortion is common, so they lump together statistics from all kinds of second- and third-term abortions, violent or not. The effect is to equate all late-term abortions with one unusual but violent and wrenching procedure. This may be good public relations, but it is dismally bad ethics.

As a result, even well-meaning people are taken in. Legislators outraged by false stories of widespread intact D&Es suggest laws to ban the procedure entirely. Most proposed laws, in turn, are so broad and so poorly worded that they might stop almost every abortion performed after the first twelve weeks of pregnancy. As the American Civil Liberties Union warns, "Because the proposed bans are worded vaguely, using non-medical terms, they could reach an array of safe and common abortion procedures."[8] The truth is clear: Abortion opponents are attempting to use the existence of a few unrepresentative intact D&E abortions as an excuse to roll back a quarter century of progress in women's rights.

The debate over partial-birth abortion is obscured by unethical activists bent on making it seem as if every late-term abortion is as violent as an intact D&E. In reality, though, the question is an easy one. In some inexpressibly tragic cases there is no valid ethical path other than to terminate a pregnancy in its latest stages. To pretend otherwise is to cause serious harm to those who desperately need the procedure. Late-term abortion, including even the intact D&E method, must remain legal.

1. "Partial Compassion," 1996. www.rcrc.org/pubs/speakout/lateterm.html.

2. Quoted in *American Medical News*, "ACOG Draws Fire for Saying Procedure 'May' Be Best Option for Some," March 3, 1997.

3. Quoted in Tamara L. Roleff, ed., *Abortion: Opposing Viewpoints*. San Diego: Greenhaven, 1997, p. 80.

4. Quoted in *American Medical News*, "ACOG Draws Fire for Saying Procedure 'May' Be Best Option for Some."

5. Quoted in Alison Landes et al., eds., *Abortion: An Eternal Social and Moral Issue*. Wylie, TX: Information Plus, 1996, p. 50.

6. Quoted in American Civil Liberties Union, "Stop Attacks on Reproductive Freedom." www.aclu.org/action/pba106.html.

7. Quoted in Baptist Message Online, "SBC Leaders Decry Recent Abortion Veto, Urge Clinton to Repent of Action," June 20, 1996. www.lacollege.edu/baptist/message/6.20.96/6.20.96.abortion.html

8. American Civil Liberties Union, "Stop Attacks on Reproductive Freedom."

*"There's a reason parents have oversight over their
children until the age of 18 . . . and it's simply absurd to
waive that oversight when it comes to the very serious
issue of abortion."*

Parental Consent Laws Are Necessary

The right to have an abortion is not absolute. The Supreme Court has ruled that states may place restrictions on women who want to obtain abortions. Among the laws of this type are ones that require teenagers to involve their parents in the abortion decision. At present about three-fifths of the states mandate teenagers seeking an abortion to get formal permission from their parents or at least to inform their families of their decision. Unaccountably, the remaining states have no such laws—unaccountably, because parental consent laws make good sense from everyone's perspective.

The most important argument in favor of these laws is that they strengthen the family—the basic unit of American society. Simply put, notification laws are good for the teenager, good for her parents, and good for the family as a whole. Lack of parental consent laws allow, perhaps even encourage, young pregnant women to push away their parents. Instead, they turn to abortionists, nurses, teachers, social workers: many of them good people, certainly, but none looking out for a girl's interests the way a parent would. The lack of parental involvement laws, mourns pro-lifer Carolyn Gargaro, tells young impressionable teenagers "that they can trust everyone EXCEPT their own parents."[1]

Parental consent laws, on the other hand, force the strengthening of family ties. A pregnant adolescent must sit down with her parents to discuss her options. This can only help the family. As state attorneys in California write, "To deny parents the opportunity [to support their daughter in a time of crisis] risks or perpetuates estrangement or alienation from the child when she is in the greatest need of parental guidance and support and denies all dignity to the family."[2]

Legal and Medical Precedents

It makes sense to require parental notification from a legal perspective, too. The age of eighteen is a significant milestone in many areas of life. People under that age need parental consent for certain activities. Minors cannot enlist in the military, for example, without their parents' consent. Minors cannot go on school trips without their parents' consent. The list goes on. Parents, in short, are legally responsible for their children's lives until the children reach age eighteen.

As a result, our society is built on parental notification. School officials do not refuse to inform parents that their children have been caught cheating on tests. Doctors do not let a fifteen-year-old patient decide whether to tell his parents that he has been in a car accident. Fifteen-year-olds—even seventeen-year-olds—lack the necessary maturity to make even these decisions for themselves. Why should abortion be different? "There's a reason parents have oversight over their children until the age of 18," writes U.S. representative Van Hilleary, "and it's simply absurd to waive that oversight when it comes to the very serious issue of abortion."[3]

What makes things even odder is that the medical community uniformly requires parental notification in virtually every other area of patient care. "Except for emergency, life-saving procedures," sums up Gargaro, doctors and hospitals "refuse treatment of a minor until a parent or guardian can be notified."[4] Surgery simply cannot be performed on a child or teenager without the consent of the parents. It is sobering to realize that this includes surgery to correct complications from an abortion—meaning that a young woman can have an abortion without her parents' knowledge but needs their approval for surgery that would fix the problems resulting from that secret operation!

Nor are consent provisions restricted to major surgery. As a California politician observes, "Parents must give consent before their child can have their ears pierced or a tattoo put on. In fact, in public schools and emergency rooms, parents must give consent before their child can be treated with so much as an aspirin."[5] Giving a girl an aspirin is not invasive; it carries few if any risks, and the effects are beneficial and occur over a period of a few hours. An abortion, on the other hand, is surgery. It destroys one life and affects another for years. Yet the aspirin must be approved by the parent, while in many states the abortion is the girl's own decision. On medical and legal grounds, it is indefensible not to require a minor to get her parents' consent before aborting.

Reduction in Abortion

The advantages of consent laws are not just philosophical. Parental consent laws significantly reduce the incidence of teen abortion. In Minnesota, for instance, abortion clinics reported a 25 percent drop in teenage abortions after consent laws were passed. Teenagers who might have aborted their babies without ever talking to their parents now talk—and the baby is more likely to be born, to grow, and to flourish under the care of its biological family or its loving adoptive parents. Even the most ardent of pro-choicers would have trouble arguing with the end result.

Furthermore, teenagers who can avoid telling their parents will be more likely to have abortions. One study cited the three most common reasons why young pregnant women had abortions without telling their parents. They were, in order, "Didn't want to hurt or disappoint parent," "Thought parent would be angry at me," and "Didn't want parent to know I was having sex."[6] Clearly, feelings of shame and embarrassment are common—as they should be. Rather than addressing these feelings and having to

talk about their actions with their families, girls in some states have an alternative: obtaining a secret abortion. Require parental consent, and communication goes up as the number of abortions drops; do not require it, and the teenage abortion rate—along with the promiscuity rate—will continue to climb.

Consent laws carry a significant benefit for the health of the young woman, too. Consider what happens in a state without such regulations. A pregnant teenager skips school, goes to an abortion clinic, has the procedure, and then, perhaps, becomes depressed, even suicidal, or develops physical problems stemming from the operation. As Gargaro points out, "Parents may not know of their child's emotional or physical pain, and they won't know to look for signs in the event that there are complications from the abortion."[7] The risks to the girl's health are obvious. So, too, is the solution: require parental consent laws.

Special Cases

There are always exceptions to rules, and even parental consent laws have their limits. Some teenagers do live in dysfunctional families. Their mothers are addicted to drugs; their fathers are absent; the parents cannot hold jobs; there is abuse. Parental consent laws should not put the abortion decision in the hands of incompetent, uncaring parents who may not have their daughters' interests at heart.

But they do not. Consent laws have safeguards, provisions that take these special cases into account. A Pennsylvania law, for example, provides that "a court may authorize the performance of an abortion upon a determination that the young women is mature and capable of giving informed consent . . . or that an abortion would be in her best interests."[8] In some states, too, grandparents may take the place of parents. The few teenagers who have good reasons to abort and good reasons not to tell their parents have nothing to fear from parental consent laws.

Parental consent laws do not place an unnecessary burden on teenagers seeking abortions: At most, they ask teenagers to ponder the question thoughtfully and with input from others older and wiser than themselves. The effects of such laws are uniformly good—they reduce abortions and perhaps even pregnancies, and they bring families closer together. Consent laws make sense from legal and medical perspectives. Even pro-choicers are revulsed by the notion of teenagers dealing with pregnancy on their own without the steadying hand of an adult. As a clinic worker says, "I don't want a fourteen-year-old coming to my clinic alone for an abortion and walking out alone after she has it. What kind of provider am I if I permit this?"[9]

And what kind of a society are we to allow very young women to choose abortion without their parents' acceptance? Parental consent laws are not a luxury. They are a necessity.

1. Carolyn Gargaro, "Protecting the Rights of Parents and Young Women—in Defense of the Child Custody Protection Act," June 12, 1998. www.gargaro.com/goodmanresponse. html.

2. Quoted in "Parental Consent or Notification for Teen Abortions: Pro and Con." www. religioustolerance.org/abo_pare.htm.

3. Van Hilleary, "Hilleary Says Parental Consent for Abortion Is Necessary," September 2, 1997. www.house.gov/hilleary.

4. Gargaro, "Protecting the Rights of Parents and Young Women."

5. "Parental Consent or Notification Laws for Teen Abortions."

6. Quoted in Alison Landes et al., eds., *Abortion: An Eternal Social and Moral Issue*. Wylie, TX: Information Plus, 1996, p. 104.

7. Gargaro, "Protecting the Rights of Parents and Young Women."

8. Quoted in Robert M. Baird and Stuart E. Rosenbaum, *The Ethics of Abortion*. Buffalo: Prometheus Books, 1993, p. 83.

9. Quoted in Marian Faux, *Crusaders: Voices from the Abortion Front*. New York: Birch Lane, 1990, p. 262.

"Enough parents do batter or abuse their daughters that consent laws will invariably endanger some children's well-being."

Parental Consent Laws Have Harmful Effects

It would be wonderful if all parents were loving and kind to their children. It would be wonderful if frightened and pregnant teenagers knew they could come to their parents for help and support. The sad fact, however, is that not all parents are able to do what is best for their children, and not all teenagers feel comfortable approaching their parents. Nor is it in the interest of every family or every teenager to force such a conversation. As a result, parental notification and consent laws, however well intentioned, are ultimately misguided and should be repealed.

Our society is far from perfect. Too many pregnant teenagers come from families in which the adults are more feared than trusted. As a lobbying group describes it, "The family is unsupportive, in crisis, dysfunctional or abusive."[1] This is not a tiny fraction of all families, as those who support parental consent laws would have it. According to a 1991 study by Stanley Henshaw and Kathryn Kost, 30 percent of the teenagers who choose not to tell their parents about their abortions do so because they fear violence or being thrown out of the family home. "Under no circumstances could she tell her father she was pregnant," a writer says of a Minnesota girl seeking an abortion. "She believed he would kill her."[2]

Not all parents threaten violence, of course. For many teenagers, parents will indeed rally around them even after the jarring news of a pregnancy. But enough parents do batter or abuse their daughters that consent laws will invariably endanger some children's well-being. How is the family bond strengthened by forcing a teenager to tell her controlling and abusive father that she wishes to have an abortion? Indeed, doing so does precisely the opposite. As one group puts it, any form of consent law "tests the already difficult relationship between parent and child, undermining the very goals it purports to promote."[3]

Family Unity?

The problems are exacerbated by the specific features of many parental consent laws. In a few states, including Arkansas, Minnesota, and Virginia, pregnant teenagers must inform both parents of their decision to abort; in a handful, such as Mississippi, both parents must actually consent to the girl's choice. Often this requires searching out a parent who has abandoned the family. The parent in question may have shown absolutely no interest in the girl's welfare since she was a toddler. Yet, as writer Marian Faux puts it, "that parent can now . . . assert his parental rights and make a decision for her that will affect the rest of her life."[4]

At best, the search for this parent takes precious time, adding to the emotional and physical stress on the young woman. At worst, it can force a teenager to give birth to a child against her will or send her into the clutches of a back-alley abortionist. These laws place a terrible burden on a girl with only the sketchiest of connections to one parent or the other. Again, it is impossible to believe that the goal of family unity is helped by such a situation.

Moreover, it is worth noting that few teenagers make the decision to abort completely on their own. Many adolescents

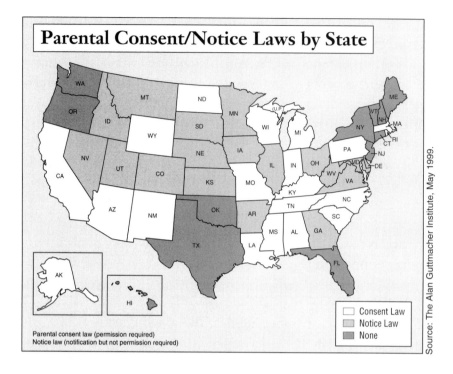

Parental Consent/Notice Laws by State

Parental consent law (permission required)
Notice law (notification but not permission required)

Consent Law
Notice Law
None

Source: The Alan Guttmacher Institute, May 1999.

have strong relationships with aunts, grandmothers, teachers, ministers, or counselors. In some cases, these relationships are more fulfilling than the relationships with the child's own parents. Yet parental consent laws rarely recognize these important connections. As the American Academy of Pediatrics (AAP) puts it, "Most notification clauses are restricted to traditional definitions of biological parents or legal guardians and fail to address the complexity and diversity of modern family structures and adult support systems relevant to adolescents."[5] Thus, the laws as written do not reflect reality; they are not in the child's best interest.

Delays

Nor is there any evidence that adolescent health is made safer by requiring parental consent. In one common scenario, a teenager required to tell her parents simply puts off the dreaded moment as long as she can—with the expected effects on her health owing to the delay. As a general rule, says the AAP, "teenagers are twice as likely as adults to delay the diagnosis of first-trimester pregnancy."[6] The situation is much worse when the girl wants an abortion. The longer the abortion is put off, the more serious the health risk for the woman. A delay of even a week significantly increases the chance of complications.

And many adolescents delay far longer than a week. In some cases, minors put off the decision until the changes in their figures are impossible to ignore. Massachusetts's notification law delayed some abortions by as much as six weeks. One study showed that Minnesota's parental notification law, while reducing legal first-trimester abortions, increased second-trimester abortions by 26.5 percent. The health risks of delaying abortion are apparent. In a few cases, delays push a pregnancy past the point where abortion is a legal, let alone safe, alternative. In the interest of young women's health, parental consent laws ought to be repealed.

The judicial bypass provisions of most consent laws do not help much, either. Few adolescents know that they can replace parental consent with the consent of a judge. Even fewer can actually get the machinery in motion to act on that knowledge. Going to a courtroom is far from easy. Poor, rural teenagers may be especially unable to make the trip. Seeking judicial help means explaining a difficult situation to a room full of strangers. Worse, some judges—the majority in several states—routinely turn down such requests. "In Indiana," writes an observer, "the judges either generally refuse to schedule hearings or are unlikely to grant approval."[7]

Moreover, judicial bypass decisions are rarely if ever handed down the same day. Days, even weeks, can pass before a decision is rendered. "Even under the best of circumstances," reports a Tennessee district court judge, "the waiver process would take twenty-two days to complete—a significant problem given the time-sensitive nature of pregnancy and the increased risk involved in later abortions."[8] For many teenagers, twenty-two days would shift the pregnancy into the next trimester—making it that much more dangerous and expensive.

Statistics

Nor is there any real evidence that parental consent laws reduce abortions. It is true that some notification laws have produced a drop in the number of abortions sought by minors in the state's clinics. However, that fact by no means implies that teenagers stopped having abortions. Some of the reduction may have come from teenagers deciding to have illegal abortions instead of telling their parents. In Mississippi, the number of teenage abortions did go down within the state. But the drop was offset entirely by a rise in the number of teenagers traveling to areas with less-restrictive laws. Consent laws should not be driving adolescents to illegal abortionists or to states far from their homes, but that is precisely their effect.

As a result of these facts, many medical organizations, including the American Medical Association, the American Academy of Pediatrics, and the American Academy of Family Physicians, have weighed in against parental notification and consent laws. Members of these organizations have observed firsthand the effects of these laws: the agony of a sixteen-year-old forced to tell her abusive father that she is pregnant, the terror of a fifteen-year-old abandoned by her parents for the crime of saying she would like to have an abortion, the conflicted seventeen-year-old who cannot quite bring herself to talk to her busy mother about her condition—while her opportunity for a safe and legal abortion diminishes every day. These doctors and nurses have been on the front lines. Their testimony cannot be denied. Parental notification and consent laws infringe on the rights of adolescents to a timely, safe abortion.

1. Quoted in "Parental Consent or Notification Laws for Teen Abortions: Pro and Con." www.religioustolerance.org/abo_pare.htm.

2. Marian Faux, *Crusaders: Voices from the Abortion Front.* New York: Birch Lane, 1990, p. 217.

3. Quoted in "Parental Consent or Notification Laws for Teen Abortions."

4. Faux, *Crusaders*, p. 216.

5. American Academy of Pediatrics, "The Adolescent's Right to Confidential Care When Considering Abortion," May 1996. www.aap.org/policy/01348.html.

6. American Academy of Pediatrics, "The Adolescent's Right to Confidential Care When Considering Abortion."

7. Quoted in Alison Landes et al., eds., *Abortion: An Eternal Social and Moral Issue*. Wylie, TX: Information Plus, 1996, p. 100.

8. Quoted in "Parental Consent or Notification Laws for Teen Abortions."

CHAPTER 4

Is Research Using Aborted Fetal Tissue Ethical?

"It is ethically abhorrent to create a baby solely so that it may be killed and its tissue used in a possibly hopeless effort to extend another person's life."

Fetal Tissue Research Is Unnecessary and Immoral

Modern science has given much to humanity, particularly in the area of health. Vaccines, antibiotics, laser surgery—all have helped to extend not only life spans but also the quality of life. But not all medical research is appropriate. A case in point is fetal tissue experimentation.

At present many scientists wish to study what happens if tissue from aborted fetuses is transplanted into people suffering from a host of chronic illnesses. Tissue from human embryos does have certain advantages over cells from humans already born: Fetal tissue can grow in new and unexpected ways, essentially helping to regenerate old and diseased body parts. The results of the testing have been far from conclusive, however. And in any case, using fetal tissue obtained from abortions is so fraught with ethical problems that we could not justify such experimentation even if the results were clear. Fetal tissue research is immoral and must be stopped.

Some early reports on fetal experiments have, in fact, been hopeful. For example, fetal tissue transplants have helped control the symptoms of a few patients with Parkinson's disease, a nerve disorder involving slow degeneration of speech and muscles. But "hopeful" is far from "certain," and "a few" is far from "all." There is simply no good evidence that these procedures work. Most fetal tissue experimentation, in fact, comes under the heading of "second-rate research."[1]

One recent study involving Parkinson's patients showed that only one in three made significant progress, and their long-term prognosis is unknown. Meanwhile, another third experienced no benefit from the grueling, invasive procedure, and some of those wound up much worse after the experiment than they had been beforehand. Yet this study, and a few similar ones, are the best supporting research that scientists can offer. Even some researchers admit, as one recently did, "the actual scientific accomplishments [have been] somewhat exaggerated."[2] To tout results like these as a triumph, as many favoring such experimentation do, is at best questionable science.

This is especially so because of serious problems with most of the studies performed to date. Competition to publish conclusions "first" has led to slipshod recordkeeping and poorly designed experiments. In the scientific world, no experimental result can be accepted until it has been duplicated and confirmed, and most fetal tissue experiments have not yet been subjected to this kind of analysis. Moreover, some researchers and their friends have too little background in this area to create good science. Philosopher Dianne N. Irving tells of a government panel, charged with the responsibility of overseeing fetal tissue research, that wound up setting policy "using amphibian embryology rather than human embryology."[3]

Besides, scientists have other alternatives. Medical science moves incredibly fast these days. As one writer puts it, " 'Eventually,' at the current pace of biotech advances, often mean[s] 'next year.' "[4] Fetal tissue is simply not necessary given such progress. Some researchers, for example, have had promising results by using patients' own cells. "From a skin biopsy the size of a quarter," says a representative of a biotechnology company, "we can produce as much tissue in two weeks as you could harvest from a hundred fetuses."[5] More and more, procedures such as these seem to be working. Couple them with possible nongenetic alternatives, and it is clear that advances are likely even without the use of fetal tissue.

Good and Evil

But even if fetal tissue research *were* good science and *did* improve many people's lives, it still would not be acceptable. The basic trouble with such research is evident by an analogy. We would not dream of curing someone's cancer by excising another human's cells against his will. Nor would we condone a heart transplant that would kill the donor, even if it might improve the length and quality of the recipient's life. Why, then, would we make an exception for the fetus?

The human rights document called the Declaration of Helsinki states, in part, "In research on man, the interests of science and society should never take precedence over considerations related to the well-being of the subject."[6] Note that no amendment adds the stipulation "unless the subject happens to be a fetus." The fetus is deserving of all the rights and safeguards we allow already-born humans—including the right not to be killed to extend or improve someone else's life.

For indeed, fetal tissue is, plain and simply, human. "[Human embryos] are human beings who are created, known, and uniquely valued by God,"[7] argues an observer. As humans, embryos are subject to the same laws and rules of ethics as the rest of us. Thus, an advocate of banning fetal tissue research asserts, "they should not be treated simply as a means to some social goal, such as improving the nation's health."[8] True, the fetus is still largely unformed, but it is human. And therefore, even if transplanting fetal tissue can cure a disease or save a life, it is still, at best, "trading one life for another."[9]

But who is to decide that a sixty-year-old man—or a thirty-five-year-old woman, for that matter—is worth "more" than a fetus? Society cannot make this judgment; nor should it. Ethical and religious systems resoundingly reject the idea that an innocent life may be taken to save someone else's. In the New Testament, to give just one example, Romans 3:8 cautions us to avoid the temptation to "do evil that good may result." At heart, the analysis of a Christian bioethical group holds: "We are not free to pursue good ends through immoral or unethical means."[10]

Encouraging More Abortions

The concern over fetal tissue research might be somewhat less if the tissue came from embryos spontaneously aborted. But it does not. Most fetal tissue used in experiments today is obtained through abortion, not through natural miscarriage. In fact, as one writer describes it, tissue from miscarriages "is usually worthless or may be diseased."[11]

That fact is cause for concern. Suppose that fetal tissue transplants could be shown to be effective treatments for a variety of relatively common diseases. Then fetal tissue would be very much in demand. Indeed, according to a pro-life observer, the demand "would far outweigh the supply . . . since each patient would require tissue from several unborn babies."[12] Doctors would take every available embryo cell for use by their patients.

Given these circumstances, it is easy to imagine the pressure on pregnant women to abort. A woman in a crisis pregnancy might be told that she need not worry about having an abortion since the cells from her embryo can help save an old man's life. A couple uncertain whether they can manage another baby will be assured that abortion is not an immoral choice since the fetus will be "recycled" to help another couple conceive.

In this scenario, abortion becomes the noble, just, even selfless thing to do. Why go through with a pregnancy when your fetus can give life to five or six leukemia patients? Even those who believe in fetal tissue experiments concede that some women "might be moved to abort by the thought that her abortion might do some good."[13] For those who believe that the fetus has an inviolable right to life, this is a chilling prospect. There is no justification for sacrificing an innocent life, no matter what the end.

"A Huge Black Market"

Moreover, fetal tissue research presents other issues. Because it permits some good to come out of abortions, society's respect for the lives of the unborn will inevitably weaken. As a right-to-life official warns, "It would affect the cultural attitude toward the unborn if society were to become hooked on this tissue."[14] In the same way, the use of fetal tissue requires a suspension of moral judgment. "Any subsequent use of the fetal tissue associates one with the immoral act,"[15] sums up a reporter; those who carry out or benefit from the experiments all are in the position of supporting abortion, even encouraging it. Abortion will be seen not as a monstrous evil but as a perfectly ordinary act that is part of normal day-to-day life.

Research on human embryos brings up a particularly thorny ethical problem, too. Supporters of fetal tissue research constantly call abortion a private and personal decision and speak in reverent tones of the woman's right to her own body, including the growing fetus inside. Thus, the aborted fetus "belongs," in some sense, to the woman who cruelly ended its life. But is this the ruling we wish to make? Surely not. Imagine the following scenario:

> What if a woman had a father with Alzheimer's Disease, a disease which totally destroys the mind and, eventually, the body of the victim? Should she be allowed to grow a fetus in her body solely for the purpose of aborting and harvesting the fetal tissue in an effort to save her father or at least to slow the progress of the disease?[16]

Most people would agree that it is ethically abhorrent to create a baby solely so that it may be killed and its tissue used in a possibly hopeless effort to extend another person's life. One does not need to be an ardent pro-lifer to see the problems here. Well-intentioned as this woman might be, she could never be morally justified in aborting her baby to help her father. But turning fetuses into commodities, as fetal tissue research does, necessarily encourages women to treat them that way—with scenarios like the one above becoming more and more common.

Worse, if these experiments are shown to work and demand for fetal tissue shoots up, human cells will be worth plenty of money. Poor women will become pregnant solely so that they can abort and sell their babies' cells. "It will create a huge black market," cautions one writer, "with the women of the Third World becoming likely targets"[17] and their innocent babies the likely victims. In a worst-case scenario, women are turned into factories, becoming pregnant and aborting in a never-ending cycle in order to add a few years to the lives of Parkinson's patients. To say that this process devalues life is to sadly understate the truth of the matter.

"This process devalues life"—that statement sums it up best. No matter what benefits fetal tissue research may offer to the infirm, society is better off taking a different road—a road that will not sacrifice one life for another, a road that will not smooth over the evils of abortion, but a road that will offer a better quality of life for all. We must steer clear of this immoral research and work toward better ways of providing for the needs of the chronically ill.

1. Quoted in Alison Landes et al., eds., *Abortion: An Eternal Social and Moral Issue.* Wylie, TX: Information Plus, 1996, p. 125.

2. Quoted in Jeff Goldberg, "Fetal Attraction," *Discover*, July 1995. www.discover.com.

3. Dianne N. Irving, "NIH and Human Embryo Research Revisited: What Is Wrong with This Picture?" www.all.org/abac/dni002.htm.

4. Gregg Easterbrook, "Medical Evolution: Will Homo Sapiens Become Obsolete?" *New Republic*, March 1, 1999.

5. Goldberg, "Fetal Attraction."

6. Quoted in Irving, "NIH and Human Embryo Research Revisited."

7. Linda Bevington, "Stem Cells and the Human Embryo: A Christian Analysis," February 5, 1999. www.bioethix.org/overviews/stemcell.html.

8. Alisdair Palmer, "We May Respect It—but We're Happy to Kill It," *Sunday Telegraph*, October 11, 1998.

9. Quoted in Tamara L. Roleff, ed., *Abortion: Opposing Viewpoints*. San Diego: Greenhaven, 1997, p. 181.

10. Bevington, "Stem Cells and the Human Embryo."

11. Quoted in Roleff, *Abortion*, p. 192.

12. Quoted in Roleff, *Abortion*, p. 182.

13. James Benedict, "The Use of Fetal Tissue," *Christian Century*, February 18, 1998, p. 165.

14. Quoted in Landes, *Abortion*, p. 125.

15. Patricia Schrock, "Fetal Tissue Transplantation," Winter 1997. www.hsc.missouri.edu/~shrp/radsci/fetal/fetal.html.

16. Landes, *Abortion*, p. 125.

17. Quoted in Roleff, *Abortion*, p. 182.

"Over 1 million fetuses are aborted each year. What is to be done with the remains? . . . Does the reverence for the fetus . . . mean dropping it into a can of medical waste— or does it mean using the valuable cells to help provide a better life for someone?"

Fetal Tissue Research Is Ethical and Will Save Lives

A great deal of time and energy has been devoted to the cause of stopping fetal tissue, or stem cell, research. Opponents of these experiments decry them as immoral and ineffective, because fetal tissue is derived from aborted fetuses. They could not be more wrong. Not only do the experiments show great promise, but the cells used in the research are not close to true human life. Moreover, the ultimate results of these experiments can improve the quality of human lives so greatly that it would, indeed, be immoral *not* to carry out the research.

Medical Advances

There can be no doubt that stem cell research holds out great hope for millions who suffer from disease. While experiments are still in the beginning stages, the research conducted thus far has been very effective in many patients afflicted with Parkinson's disease and several other disabling conditions. "The improvement has been spectacular" in a few Parkinson's patients, writes a reporter. After receiving transplants of fetal nerve cells, the patients "regained a range of mobility they thought they had lost forever."[1] One patient has resumed cross-country skiing. Another had been "embarrassed to eat with friends because he could no longer feed himself properly," but "celebrated the one-year anniversary of his transplant with a Thanksgiving dinner for 12."[2]

True, not every patient has responded the same way, but that is an argument to do more such research, not less. We need to know *why* some patients do not respond. We need to understand precisely *how* the tissue works to regenerate dead and dying cells in the human body. With further experiments, perhaps scientists can find a way to make the transplants work for all Parkinson's sufferers.

Similar arguments apply to a host of other illnesses, including diabetes, Huntington's chorea, and heart disease, to name a few. As a general rule, any condition caused by the failure of human cells to work properly may be treatable through fetal tissue transplants. That may cover even accidental injuries, such as those to the spinal cord. In one intriguing experiment, fetal tissue was transplanted into partially paralyzed cats. "Some of the cats began walking again," a writer summarizes. "One could even climb stairs."[3] As one researcher concludes, fetal tissue is simply "too valuable not to use in a research or therapeutic setting."[4]

Birth Defects and Fertility

And fetal research may lead to still more knowledge. Already some scientists are studying how to use fetuses to prevent birth defects. "A fetus with sickle cell anemia, for instance," writes a reporter, "could be treated with a transplant of a snippet from a fetal liver—eliminating the need for a [risky and painful] bone marrow transplant after birth."[5] Such transplants have already worked on a few patients. The behavior of fetal tissue may likewise shed light on the causes and characteristics of cancer. "Because of the embryo's mysterious capacity for rapid but controlled cell division," writes a research advocate, "scientists think it may yield clues to stopping a disease [that is, cancer] in which cell growth runs out of control."[6]

Yet another use for fetal cells is so-called fetal ovary transplantation, in which ovarian tissue from fetuses is implanted in the womb of a sterile woman, thus rendering her fertile. What could be more pro-family and pro-life than helping infertile couples produce their own families? It is odd to see self-described pro-lifers battling this use of fetal tissue. In this case, research simply *produces* and *improves* life.

Clearly, fetal tissue research promises great changes in the quality of life for many people. These experiments may help thousands avoid blindness, paralysis, senility, and strokes. Despite the very real risks of participating in such experimental research, Parkinson's patients have clamored to be included in trials: They are willing to endure much pain and uncertainty in exchange for the prospect of staving off a dismal future. How can we tell these desperate people that our society will not allow them to benefit from the one thing that may cure them?

The answer is that we cannot. Ethically, we cannot sit idly by and watch as a Parkinson's patient slips further into disability and incoherence, as a diabetic slowly goes blind, as a woman with a heart condition approaches the day when her heart will no longer work. Doing so would be a great evil. In the future new cures may be found for these patients, treatments that do not rely on human embryos. However, we have not yet reached that day. As a medical group puts it, "Fetal tissue transplantation will be a vital part of cellular therapy in years to come."[7] The benefits of fetal tissue research are enormous—so enormous, in fact, that it would be unethical to forbid it.

Not Truly Human

Antiresearch groups argue that the ethical benefits of such research are outweighed by the evils of the source of the cells—

aborted fetuses. Certainly, we must think long and hard about the moral issues involved in using aborted human fetuses for research purposes. The fetus *is* worthy of respect; it is a potential human life, not a computer simulation nor even a laboratory rat. Still, the respect due to a fetus cannot be compared with the respect due to a living, thinking, breathing human being. "We should respect every embryo," agrees a bioethicist, "but I'm not going to look at a person in a wheelchair and say, 'Sorry, you have to stay in that wheelchair for the rest of your life'"[8] because the fetus's rights are more important.

It must be understood, first of all, that the cells on which experiments are carried out are not truly human. Some embryos brought to the laboratory for research purposes are unimaginably tiny. As one writer puts it, they are "no bigger than the period at the end of this sentence."[9] The fetuses obtained from early abortions are not at all well developed. They do not breathe, they do not feel pain, their organs are rudimentary, they cannot possibly exist outside the womb.

Fetal cells are thus at best potential humans, not actual humans. Even their potential human existence is something of an overstatement since up to a third of all fertilized eggs are miscarried by natural means. To put these bundles of undeveloped cells on a moral plane with truly developed human adults, children, and babies is unjustified. Thus, as one observer argues, "Research on embryos and fetuses . . . does not cause indignity to human life. On the contrary, it dignifies life by perhaps helping to save others."[10]

Organ Donations

The fact that aborted fetuses are the source of fetal cells, however, does present potentially troubling issues. "It is not plausible to maintain that there is nothing morally problematic about abortion,"[11] admits an ethicist who supports cell research. One need not be a pro-lifer to fear that abortion may, in some way, be legitimized or even encouraged by the need for fetal tissue. However, these worries are greatly exaggerated; the concerns are either not realistic, or they can be taken care of easily and quickly.

First, abortion, at present, is a fact of life. It is legal, it is widespread, and it shows no signs of going away any time soon. Over 1 million fetuses are aborted each year. What is to be done with the remains? Except as publicity stunts, virtually no one gives fetal tissue burial and memorial services as they would for a fully formed human being. Does true reverence for the fetus, then, mean dropping it into a can of medical waste, or does it mean using the valuable cells to help provide a better life for someone? Clearly, research is the most ethical use of aborted fetal tissue.

In this way, fetal tissue transplants are much like organ donations. We accept organ donations, and accept them gratefully, regardless of the way in which they were obtained. Similarly, one need not like, or support, abortion in order to reap the benefits from stem cell research. "Use of fetal tissue," sums up an observer, "does not imply approval of past abortions or encouragement of future abortions, any more than the transplantation of a heart or kidney implies approval of—or encourages—drunk driving, domestic violence or drive-by shootings."[12]

The analogy extends still further. No one argues against safety measures such as seat-belt laws and gun control because they might lower organ donation rates. On the contrary, we continue to try to make the world a safer place while making the best possible use of the tragedies that nevertheless result. The same argument covers abortion and stem cell research. We can continue to work against the solution of abortion, regardless of the effect on the supply of stem cells, while using the products of the abortion to improve the quality of life among the living.

Safeguards

In any case, the fears that such research encourages abortion seem overly dramatic and unrealistic. In one study of Canadian women, only about one in eight said that she would be "more likely to have an abortion" if she "knew that the tissue from the fetus could be used to help someone suffering from Parkinson's disease."[13] Many ethicists think even this figure seriously overstates matters. "The physical and emotional risks of abortion are simply too great"[14] for women to be influenced by altruism, argues one observer; another says flatly that "research on already aborted fetuses does not cause women to have abortions."[15] Indeed, a 1993 study by the National Institutes of Health (NIH) Advisory Panel found absolutely no evidence that women were having abortions for altruistic reasons.

And much concern could be dispelled with a few sensible guidelines, many of which are already in place as NIH rules. Require complete anonymity between the woman who donates the fetus and the recipient. Make it clear that the fetus is not the property of the woman, so she cannot determine where the cells will go. Forbid payments of any sort for fetal tissue. Finally, as one writer puts it, there must be "a clear separation between abortion counseling and management of fetal tissue harvesting"[16]—that is, women must not be encouraged to provide fetal tissue for research until after they have made the decision to abort.

With these guidelines in place, it would not be possible to argue that stem cell research encourages abortion. The fact of the matter is that fetal research is the best response to the tragedy of abortion. A true pro-lifer must recognize this. Fetal tissue experiments are not ideal; far from it. But they are ethical and desirable given the realities of the world in which we live. As a minister points out,

> We should vigorously pursue the research and development of treatment options that may decrease or replace the use of fetal tissue. . . . We should hope for and work toward a time in which the use of tissue from elective abortions is replaced by other treatments. But

meanwhile we must live with respect and compassion in this time when fetal tissue is the last, best, or only hope for some.[17]

1. Traci Watson, "A Tissue of Promises," *U.S. News & World Report*, August 8, 1994, p. 50.

2. Jeff Goldberg, "Fetal Attraction," *Discover*, July 1995.

3. Watson, "A Tissue of Promises," p. 50.

4. Quoted in Patricia Schrock, "Fetal Tissue Transplantation," Winter 1997. www.hsc.missouri.edu/~shrp/radsci/fetal/fetal.html.

5. Watson, "A Tissue of Promises," p. 51.

6. Meredith Wadman, "Embryo Research Is Pro-Life," *New York Times*, February 21, 1996, p. A15.

7. Quoted in Schrock, "Fetal Tissue Transplantation."

8. Quoted in Gregg Easterbrook, "Medical Evolution: Will Homo Sapiens Become Obsolete?" *New Republic*, March 1, 1999.

9. Wadman, "Embryo Research Is Pro-Life," p. A15.

10. Dorothy C. Wertz, "Human Embryonic Stem Cells: A Source of Organ Transplants," *Gene Letter*, February 1999. http://geneletter.org/0299/HumanEmbryonicStemCells.htm.

11. Quoted in Tamara L. Roleff, ed., *Abortion: Opposing Viewpoints.* San Diego: Greenhaven, 1997, p. 185.

12. James Benedict, "The Use of Fetal Tissue," *Christian Century*, February 18, 1998, p. 164.

13. Quoted in Roleff, *Abortion*, p. 182.

14. Benedict, "The Use of Fetal Tissue," p. 165.

15. Wertz, "Human Embryonic Stem Cells."

16. Schrock, "Fetal Tissue Transplantation."

17. Quoted in Benedict, "The Use of Fetal Tissue," p. 165.

STUDY QUESTIONS

Chapter 1

1. Both viewpoints use evidence from biology and from religious tradition. Which type of evidence do you find most compelling? Explain why, giving examples.

2. Is it reasonable for a person to believe that abortion is murder and yet argue that it should be legal? Explain your answer, citing examples from the text and the documents.

3. Which side might bring up the fact that identical twins spring from the same egg after fertilization? Why might this evidence be helpful to their cause? How might a supporter of the other side respond?

4. Many cultures, especially in ancient times, permitted infanticide, or the killing of babies already born. How would a pro-life person use this fact to argue that abortion is murder? How would a pro-choice person use it to argue that abortion is not murder?

Chapter 2

1. Which of the arguments in this chapter are based on practicality? Which are based on morality? Which do you find most successful? Explain why.

2. What assumptions do right-to-lifers make about the motives of women who seek abortions? How do pro-choice supporters respond?

Chapter 3

1. Much of the debate about partial-birth abortion centers on the exact meaning of that term. What other assumptions are made— and not shared—by those who believe the procedure should be banned and those who believe it should be legal?

2. Some parents do raise and enjoy multiply handicapped children. How would someone who believes that birth defects are a reasonable cause for abortion respond to this fact?

3. What do those who accept Viewpoint 3 think about family life in America today? How is this perspective different from the ideas of those who accept Viewpoint 4?

4. Some states require that women who wish to have an abortion wait twenty-four hours between saying so to a provider and ac-

tually undergoing the procedure. Is this requirement more or less invasive than parental notification and consent? Why?

5. Supporters of parental notification and consent laws say that other procedures and activities already require parental consent. Opponents respond that abortion is more complicated and therefore different. Which argument do you find more compelling? Why?

Chapter 4

1. To what extent is this debate an argument about abortion? What other considerations are there? Explain your answer, giving examples from the viewpoints.

2. What assumptions about abortion are made by those who agree with the first viewpoint? How do these assumptions relate to the viewpoints given in the first two chapters?

3. Some of the debate in this chapter centers on the question of whether one life can ever be ethically "traded" for another. Under what circumstances, if any, do you believe that this can be done? Explain your answer.

APPENDIX A

Facts About Abortion

—Reported legal abortions in the United States, 1972: 586,760

—Estimated illegal abortions in the United States, 1972: 200,000–1 million.

—Reported legal abortions in the United States, 1995: 1,210,883

—As of 1998, about 35 million legal abortions have been performed in the United States since *Roe v. Wade*.

—For all American women, about 24 percent of pregnancies end in abortion. For teenagers, the rate is about 41 percent.

—About 60 percent of abortions are performed on white women, 35 percent on African American women.

—About 20 percent of abortions are performed on married women.

—About 20 percent of abortions are performed on teenagers. About a third of abortions are performed on women aged twenty to twenty-four.

—About 88 percent of abortions are performed during the first trimester. A little over 1 percent of abortions involve third-trimester pregnancies.

—As of 1998, thirty states had laws requiring either parental notification or consent in the case of minors. (Note: States frequently change their laws, and some are more selective in enforcement than others.)

—The United States has approximately one thousand abortion providers; however, 85 percent of counties have no abortion provider.

—Twelve percent of American medical schools teach abortion.

—About one of every one hundred thousand women who undergoes an abortion dies from the surgery.

APPENDIX B

Excerpts from Related Documents

Document 1: Life Begins at Fertilization

In this excerpt from New Perspectives on Human Abortion, *edited by Thomas W. Hilgers et al., the group Scientists for Life traces a direct path backward to argue that life begins at fertilization.*

Before you were an adult, you were an adolescent, and before that a child, and before that an infant. Before you were an infant—i. e. before you were born—you were a fetus, and before that an embryo. Before you were an embryo, around the time of your implantation [into the womb], you were a blastocyst, and before that a morula, and before that a zygote or fertilized ovum. However, you were never a sperm or an unfertilized ovum. Therefore, while life is continuous, your life began when the nucleus of your father's sperm fused with the nucleus of your mother's ovum, or at fertilization.

Document 2: The Fetus Is Not a Person

In this excerpt from Decoding Abortion Rhetoric, *author Celeste Michelle Condit points out the traditional differences in law and society between fetuses and children who have been born.*

American society has systematically treated a fetus as different from a person. [Laws and] custom [have] treated the fetus differently. Persons in our society have names, and we have never given fetuses names. The naming as a unique individual person occurs at birth. Additionally, persons in our society are given ritualized burials, but outside of the Catholic church (and even here, by necessity, the fetus is treated somewhat differently), miscarriages have not generally been given the same funeral and burial customary in the society.

Document 3: "This Child Feels Pain"

One of the most controversial films of the year 1984 was an antiabortion movie called Silent Scream, *which purported to be actual ultrasound footage of an abortion. Dr. Bernard Nathanson, a former abortion provider, stopped doing abortions after making and narrating the movie. In this excerpt, reprinted in editor Bonnie Szumski's* Abortion: Opposing Viewpoints, *he explains why.*

You can see from the moment the tip of the suction machine starts to move, the fetus knows it and starts to scuttle to the top of the uterus. You can see her mouth open in a silent scream. From there on you can see all the agitation: you can see the heart speeding up, you can see the limbs moving faster, you can see the child moving more rapidly. Even the breathing increases. So there is no question this child feels pain, and actually senses danger.

Document 4: The "Right to Life"

Philosophers often debate the abortion question by finding analogous situations. In The Rights and Wrongs of Abortion, *edited by Marshall Cohen et al., ethicist Judith Jarvis Thomson uses an analogy to argue that the fetus does not have an inalienable "right to life."*

In some views having a right to life includes having a right to be given at least the bare minimum one needs for continued life. But suppose that what in fact *is* the bare minimum a man needs for continued life is something he has no right at all to be given. If I am sick unto death, and the only thing that will save my life is the touch of [actor] Henry Fonda's cool hand on my fevered brow, then all the same, I have no right to be given the touch of Henry Fonda's cool hand on my fevered brow. It would be frightfully nice of him to fly in from the West Coast to provide it. It would be less nice, though no doubt well meant, if my friends flew out to the West Coast and carried Henry Fonda back with them. But I have no right at all . . . that he should do this for me.

Document 5: "Maimed for Life"

The pro-choice movement often refers to the days of illegal abortions in order to make two points: that women will get abortions, regardless of whether they are legal, and that illegal abortion was extremely risky to women's lives and health. This passage, from a Planned Parenthood brochure, which is reprinted in editor Bonnie Szumski's Abortion: Opposing Viewpoints, *explains the issues.*

If you wonder whether legal abortion is a good idea, ask any woman who survived an illegal one.

She'll tell you how painful, dirty, humiliating, and horribly dangerous a back-alley abortion was.

But despite the incredible risks, millions of American women had abortions before they were legalized nationwide in 1973. An untold number were maimed for life. Thousands were literally slaughtered, packed off bleeding and infected to die in abject terror.

Today the threat to women's lives no longer comes from abortion. It comes from those who want to outlaw it. People who argue that abortions should be banned—even if the result will be as horrifying as it was in the past.

Document 6: *Roe v. Wade*

Justice Harry Blackmun wrote the majority opinion for Roe v. Wade, *the case that won the right to a first-trimester abortion on a national level. Blackmun's summary of the argument used to determine the point at which the state could regulate abortions is excerpted from* The Ethics of Abortion, *edited by Robert M. Baird and Stuart E. Rosenbaum.*

With respect to the State's important and legitimate interest in potential life, the "compelling" point is at viability. This is so because the fetus then presumably has the capability of meaningful life outside the mother's womb. State regulation protective of fetal life after viability thus has both logical and biological justifications. If the State is interested in protecting fetal life after viability, it may go so far as to proscribe abortion during that period, except where it is necessary to preserve the life and health of the mother.

Document 7: Abortion Masks More Significant Problems in Society

Pro-lifers believe that easy access to abortion is not helpful to society, arguing that the underlying conflicts making life difficult for a woman or a family will not go away just because a fetus is aborted. Two pro-life researchers explore this argument in New Perspectives on Human Abortion, *edited by Thomas W. Hilgers et al.*

Abortion cannot be considered a real form of help for the pregnant woman because, while she may be able to talk herself into undergoing the procedure, her emotional conflicts will probably not go away with her child. Her ambivalence will remain, and it may well become a torturing guilt once the opportunity to keep the child is gone. Besides, the circumstances that lead her to abortion are unlikely to change, especially the circumstance of poverty; cruelest of all, those who were so kind and ready to give her support during her decision may well refuse to help her now, leaving her alone to carry the burden of guilt and sorrow.

Document 8: "Why Do So Many Women Do It?"

Supporters of abortion rights also argue that abortion is a social problem. In this excerpt from Marian Faux's Crusaders: Voices from the Abortion Front, *Frances Kissling of Catholics for a Free Choice questions standard pro-life explanations for the prevalence of abortion.*

What must the pro-life people think of women if they believe that women will go out and kill their own kids? What kind of horrifying notion of humanity is that? These people see humanity as horrifyingly, totally corrupted. . . . We have to ask what is wrong with a world that makes women go out and have so many abortions. It is an inadequate explanation to say that women are selfish. That doesn't begin to explain the horror or the magnitude of the pro-life movement's objections to abortion. We need to challenge these folks to get on with it, to tell us what would drive a woman to do this thing they consider so awful? Why do so many women do it? We need to say to them, if you really see abortion as the mass murder of innocents, then understand that your approach to it, making it illegal, is only a drop in the bucket toward solving the problem. If this world is so corrupted, so desensitized as to murder its children, then the solution is nothing less than a radical transformation of society so that women won't feel they have to do this.

Document 9: Abortion Is Helpful to Women

A common theme in much pro-choice literature is that easy access to abortion is necessary for true equality between the sexes. This excerpt from a 1982 book called

The Abortion Guide, *which was reprinted in editor Bonnie Szumski's* Abortion: Opposing Viewpoints, *addresses this argument.*

We know that for the very young abortion may mean the difference between continuing school or dropping out. It may mean the difference between welfare and self-sufficiency. It may mean not having to suffer the pain of giving a child away. Abortion will allow others to pursue careers or prevent forced marriages. It can make the difference between adequate and inadequate nutrition, clothing, and shelter. For some it will mean not having to bear a rapist's or relative's baby. It can preserve the physical health and sometimes the lives of women who have chronic illness or disease. It can preserve the mental health of those hovering on the brink of breakdowns. It can prevent the birth of children doomed to die.

Document 10: Abortion Is Antifeminist

Some feminists have challenged the notion that abortion is helpful to women. In this excerpt from The Ethics of Abortion, *edited by Robert M. Baird and Stuart E. Rosenbaum, psychologist and self-described "pro-life feminist" Sydney Callahan argues that pro-choice rhetoric is ultimately harmful to women.*

Society in general, and men in particular, have to provide women more support in rearing the next generation, or our devastating feminization of poverty will continue. But if a woman claims the right to decide by herself whether the fetus becomes a child or not, what does this do to paternal and communal responsibility? Why should men share responsibility for child support or childrearing if they cannot share in what is asserted to be the woman's sole decision? . . .

For that matter, why should the state provide a system of day-care or child support, or require workplaces to accommodate women's maternity and the needs of childrearing? Permissive abortion, granted in the name of women's privacy and reproductive freedom, ratifies the view that pregnancies and children are a woman's private individual responsibility.

Document 11: Restrictions on Abortion

In 1992, the Supreme Court restricted some abortion rights in its decision in Planned Parenthood of Southeastern Pennsylvania v. Casey. *Pennsylvania had placed various restrictions on first-trimester abortions, notably twenty-four-hour waiting periods, parental consent laws, and the requirement that married women tell their husbands. The decision upheld* Roe v. Wade *while also upholding most parts of the Pennsylvania law (though not the husband notification section). Editors Robert M. Baird and Stuart E. Rosenbaum quote the Court's decision in their book* The Ethics of Abortion.

It is a constitutional liberty of the woman to have some freedom to terminate her pregnancy. We conclude that the basic decision in *Roe* was based on a constitutional analysis which we cannot now repudiate. The woman's liberty is not so unlimited, however, that from the outset the State cannot show its concern for the life of the unborn, and at a later point in fetal development the State's interest in life has sufficient force so that the right of the woman to terminate the pregnancy can be restricted.

Document 12: Abortion and Rape

Sandra Mahkorn, who has studied women who have become pregnant as a result of rape, believes that society too often pushes these women to have abortions even when this may not be the best solution. Her statement is excerpted from New Perspectives on Human Abortion, *edited by Thomas W. Hilgers et al.*

Perhaps as a result of their own biases or an unwillingness to deal with the more emotionally difficult and demanding complications of a pregnant victim, many physicians curtly dismiss the issue by prescribing abortion in these cases as one would prescribe aspirin, fluids, and bed rest for a cold. Ironically, those purporting to promote respect for the sexual assault victim too often propose a paternalistic attitude when the question of pregnancy arises. A sensitive awareness of the individual is abandoned with many of the so-called quick and easy solutions. . . .

In the majority of these cases, it appears that the pregnant victim's problems stem more from the trauma of rape rather than from the pregnancy itself.

Document 13: Parental Consent for Abortion Is Necessary

In the article "Hilleary Says Parental Consent for Abortion Is Necessary," U.S. representative Van Hilleary of Tennessee argues that parental notification laws are common sense. He is writing directly after a state consent law was blocked by federal judge John T. Nixon.

We, as a nation, have determined that children under the age of 16 are not ready to drive a car on their own and children under 18 are not ready to make the decision about whether or not to smoke cigarettes. People under the age of 21 are not allowed to drink alcoholic beverages. Parents must even give their permission before high school students can go on a road trip to a museum, and often before their children can get their ears pierced.

But when Judge Nixon struck down the parental consent law for abortion, he was effectively saying, "A 15-year-old girl is NOT mature enough to get her ears pierced or get an aspirin at school without parental consent. She's not old enough to smoke cigarettes, to drive a car, or to go on a school road trip without a signed permission slip. But if she wants to make the life-or-death decision to have an abortion, that's fine."

Document 14: "A Pleasant Fantasy"

In this excerpt from Crusaders: Voices from the Abortion Front, *writer Marian Faux argues that parental consent and notification laws, while well intentioned, are flawed.*

The notion that our children will come to us with their problems is mostly a pleasant fantasy, mental health experts tell us. The fact is, few of us come from the kind of happy home that exists in television sit-coms, and those of us who are lucky enough to have been brought up in such an environment must imagine what life is like for the pregnant teen who lacks this support system. A teen-ager who refuses to tell her parents she is pregnant usually has a good reason for not doing so: She fears the anger of an alcoholic or drug-addicted parent; she fears physical violence; she may even fear for her life. Or she may be pregnant as the result of an incestuous relationship with the father whose consent she must now seek.

Document 15: The Potential Benefits of Stem Cell Research

In his article "Medical Evolution: Will Homo Sapiens Become Obsolete?" journalist Gregg Easterbrook describes some of the potential benefits of stem cell research for the ill—and ultimately for everybody.

If researchers can convert stem cells into regular cells like blood or heart muscle and then put them back in the body, then physicians might cure Parkinson's, diabetes, leukemia, heart congestion, and many other maladies, replacing failing cells with brand-new tissue. Costly afflictive procedures such as bone-marrow transplants might become easier and cheaper with the arrival of stem-cell-based "universal donor" tissue that does not provoke the immune-rejection response. The need for donor organs for heart or liver transplants might fade, as new body parts are cultured artificially. Ultimately, mastery of the stem cell might lead to practical, affordable ways to eliminate many genetic diseases through DNA engineering, while extending the human life span. Our near descendants might live in a world in which such killers as cystic fibrosis and sickle-cell anemia are one-in-a-million conditions, while additional decades of life are the norm.

Granted, sensational promises made for new medical technologies don't always come to pass, and some researchers are skeptical about whether stem-cell technology will pan out. But Harold Varmus, head of the National Institutes of Health (NIH), recently declared, "This research has the potential to revolutionize the practice of medicine." Notes John Fletcher, a bioethicist at the University of Virginia, "Soon every parent whose child has diabetes or any cell-failure disease is going to be riveted to this research, because it's the answer." Ron McKay, a stem-cell researcher at the National Institute of Neurological Disorders and Stroke, says, "We are now at the center of biology itself." Simply put, the control of human stem cells may open the door to the greatest medical discovery since antibiotics.

Document 16: Using Fetal Tissue for Research
Is Unnecessary and Immoral

Some opponents of fetal tissue research argue that there are many effective alternatives to fetus-based treatments; all that is wanting is sufficient study. This ex-

cerpt from Linda Bevington's article "Stem Cells and the Human Embryo: A Christian Analysis," appearing on the website of The Center for Bioethics and Human Dignity, a Christian group, is a sample.

Shouldn't it be ethical to allow the destruction of a few embryos in order to help the millions of people who suffer from diseases such as Parkinson's and heart disease? Many proponents of human embryonic stem cell research argue that it is actually wrong to protect the lives of a few unborn human beings if doing so will delay treatment for a much larger number of people who suffer from fatal or debilitating diseases. However, we are not free to pursue good ends through immoral or unethical means (Deut. 27:25). The medical experiments in Nazi Germany should serve as just one reminder of the consequences of doing evil in the name of science. We must not sacrifice one class of human beings (the embryonic) to benefit another (those suffering from serious illness). Scripture resoundingly rejects the temptation to "do evil that good may result" (Romans 3:8).

Does all stem cell research involve the destruction of human embryos or the use of aborted fetal tissue? The National Bioethics Advisory Commission (NBAC) has identified many potential avenues of stem cell research which would not involve the use of human embryos. Included in these are techniques which would stimulate the growth and specialization of stem cells found in adult tissues and the use of stem cells from bone marrow or umbilical cord blood. Recent scientific breakthroughs have demonstrated that the destruction of embryos may indeed not be at all necessary to achieve the benefits promised by stem cell research. Federal funds should be allotted to develop these alternative methods of stem cell research rather than those which require embryo destruction—even if the latter promises more rapid medical advances.

Is the government now funding the destruction of embryos? The Department of Health and Human Services (DHHS) has determined that federal funds may legally be used to support research on human embryonic stem cells. Although federal funds may not be used to finance the destruction of embryos which occurs when the stem cells are obtained, this technicality is overcome by ensuring that embryo-derived stem cells are procured by privately-funded scientists, who in turn provide them to federally-funded researchers for experimentation. Because those who fund and carry out such research are in effect sanctioning the destruction of embryonic human life, they are also guilty of immoral action.

Document 17: Fetal Tissue Research Is Appropriate

In this excerpt from editor Tamara L. Roleff's Abortion: Opposing View-points, *medical ethicist Carson Strong argues that the benefits that fetal tissue research offers the living outweigh the problems it brings.*

It can be argued that the potential for benefit from fetal tissue transplantation is morally significant. Those who might benefit—sufferers of Parkinson's disease, diabetes, and other disabling disorders—are indeed persons, a fact that is absolutely without controversy. Thus, if there is a benefit to those individuals, it will undoubtedly have moral significance because it is a benefit to persons. Moreover, there is a reasonable chance that there will be at least some benefit from going forward with this area of clinical research. Even if it turns out that fetal tissue transplantation does not provide effective treatments, knowledge will be gained about the human body, disease, and therapeutic interventions. Such knowledge often has a way of eventually contributing, in greater or less degree, to the development of useful applications. In addition, if therapies prove effective, the degree of the benefits might be great.

In summary, transplantation and research involving human fetal tissue appear ethically justifiable because the degree of wrongness that might be involved seems relatively low, no rights would be violated (assuming the woman having the abortion gives informed consent to use of the fetal tissue, and other pertinent guidelines and law as are followed), at least some benefit is reasonably expected, and great benefits are possible.

Document 18: Abortion Is a Difficult Problem

While some people involved in the abortion debate vehemently take one side or the other, many more waver, agreeing in some cases with pro-lifers, other times with pro-choicers. This excerpt from the 1976 United Methodist Church's General Conference, reprinted in New Perspectives on Human Abortion, *edited by Thomas W. Hilgers et al., the church explains its discomfort with both extremes.*

When, through contraceptive or human failure, an unacceptable pregnancy occurs, we believe that a profound regard for unborn human life must be weighed alongside an equally profound regard for fully developed personhood, particularly when the physical, mental and emotional health of the pregnant woman and her family show reason to be seriously threatened by the new life just forming. We reject the simplistic answers to the problem of abortion, which on the one hand regard all abortions as murders, or on the other hand, regard abortions as medical procedures without moral significance.

ORGANIZATIONS TO CONTACT

The editors have compiled the following list of organizations concerned with the issues debated in this book. The descriptions are derived from materials provided by the organizations. All have publications or information available for interested readers. The list was compiled on the date of publication of the present volume; the information provided here may change. Be aware that many organizations take several weeks or longer to respond to inquiries, so allow as much time as possible.

Alan Guttmacher Institute
120 Wall St., 21st Fl.
New York, NY 10005
(212) 248-1111
Website: www.agi-usa.org/home.html

An advocacy group that aims to keep abortion safe and legal, the institute provides publications and conducts research into issues surrounding pregnancy, abortion, and population control.

American Civil Liberties Union (ACLU)
125 Broad St., 18th Fl.
New York, NY 10004-2400
(212) 549-2500
Website: www.aclu.org

The ACLU's purpose is to uphold the Bill of Rights—the Constitutional amendments that protect citizens against unwarranted governmental control. Traditionally, abortion rights have been among the rights that the ACLU strives to protect.

American Life League
PO Box 1350
Stafford, VA 22555
(540) 659-4171
Website: www.all.org

The American Life League opposes abortion and embraces a pro-family stance toward most issues. It seeks to educate and inform the public about the risks of abortion, both in terms of physical and mental health.

Birthright USA
National Office
PO Box 98363
Atlanta, GA 30359-2063
(800) 550-4900
Website: www.birthright.org

Birthright USA is part of Birthright International, an organization founded in 1968 to provide support services for women distressed by pregnancy. The organization is pro-life; its slogan is "It is the right of every pregnant woman to give birth, and the right of every child to be born."

Catholics for a Free Choice
1436 U St. NW, Suite 301
Washington, DC 20009-3997
(202) 986-6093
Website: www.cath4choice.org

Catholics for a Free Choice is a pro-choice Roman Catholic organization involved in education, advocacy, and analysis. It also works toward greater gender equity in the Church and in society. The organization's roots are in the long-standing tradition of Catholic social justice.

Center for Bio-Ethical Reform
PO Box 8056
Mission Hills, CA 91346
(818) 360-2477
Website: www.cbrinfo.org/index.html

This group is a pro-life organization that works from the assumption that the fetus is fully human. Its mission also includes protecting the right to life of people who are old, disabled, or infirm; it opposes violence of all kinds, including clinic violence.

National Abortion and Reproductive Rights Action League (NARAL)
1156 15th St. NW, Suite 700
Washington, DC 20005
(202) 973-3000
Website: www.naral.org/home.html

An organization dedicated to preserving abortion rights, NARAL offers publications, gets involved in political action, and works to educate Americans on the issues surrounding abortion.

National Conference of Catholic Bishops (NCCB)
3211 Fourth St. NE
Washington, DC 20017
(202) 541-3000
Website: www.nccbuscc.org
The official mouthpiece of American Roman Catholic bishops, the NCCB supports the pro-life stance of the Vatican. It issues publications and lobbies state and federal governments to ban abortion or restrict it.

National Organization for Women (NOW)
1000 16th St. NW, Suite 700
Washington, DC 20036
(202) 331-0066
Website: www.now.org

This group focuses on feminism and women's rights. Open access to abortion is a major thrust of NOW's political and educational activities.

National Right to Life Committee
419 Seventh St. NW, Suite 500
Washington, DC 20004
(202) 626-8800
Website: www.nrlc.org

This group advocates against abortion. In the past it has campaigned for constitutional changes that would outlaw the practice; it also encourages alternatives to abortion, such as adoption. It is among the largest pro-life organizations in the nation.

Planned Parenthood Federation of America
810 Seventh Ave.
New York, NY 10019
(212) 541-7800
Website: www.plannedparenthood.org

Perhaps the best known of all pro-choice organizations, Planned Parenthood offers abortion and family planning services at clinics across the country. It lobbies for the right of women to have an abortion without interference from the government.

Religious Coalition for Reproductive Choice
1025 Vermont Ave. NW, Suite 1130
Washington, DC 20005
(202) 628-7700
Website: www.rcrc.org

This group is made up of pro-choice religious organizations that believe that abortion can be within the compass of morality. The coalition is especially involved in opposition to clinic violence and in educating people about the variety of religious opinion on abortion.

FOR FURTHER READING

Claudia M. Caruana, *The Abortion Debate*. Brookfield, CT: Mill-brook, 1992. An even-handed history of abortion, abortion rights, and the various positions taken by different groups on the legal and moral issues at the heart of the debate.

Nancy Day, *Abortion: Debating the Issue*. Springfield, NJ: Enslow, 1995. Intended specifically for young adults, this book explores some of the controversies in the abortion debate today, including clinic violence and the question of morality.

Marian Faux, *Crusaders: Voices from the Abortion Front*. New York: Birch Lane, 1990. A journalistic account. Faux interviewed a number of abortion providers, activists, and opponents. This book tells what she learned, often in the subjects' own words.

Susan Dudley Gold, *Roe v. Wade*. New York: Twenty First Century Books, 1995. A book focusing on the case that made abortion legal in all states, including background on the time period and information about the impact of the decision.

Joann B. Guernsey, *Abortion: Understanding the Controversy*. Minneapolis: Lerner, 1993. A consideration of the biological, ethical, and moral issues surrounding abortion and abortion rights.

Charles Panati, *Sacred Origins of Profound Things*. New York: Penguin Books USA, 1996. A fascinating book giving the background and development of many religious rituals and doctrines, including a section on Catholicism and abortion.

Tamara L. Roleff, ed., *Abortion: Opposing Viewpoints*. San Diego: Greenhaven, 1997. Excerpts from books, articles, and opinion pieces representing many different perspectives on abortion. Includes study guides and useful appendices.

Bonnie Szumski, ed., *Abortion: Opposing Viewpoints*. San Diego: Greenhaven, 1986. An earlier version of the Roleff book mentioned above, with entirely different documents and several different arguments.

John W. Wright, ed., *The New York Times Almanac 1999*. New York: Penguin Reference Books, 1998. A book of facts and general information, including statistics on abortions.

Works Consulted

Books

Randy Alcorn, *Pro-Life Answers to Pro-Choice Arguments*. Portland, OR: Multnomah, 1992. As the title suggests, a discussion of the differences between the pro-choice and pro-life perspectives, with an emphasis on the latter.

Robert M. Baird and Stuart E. Rosenbaum, *The Ethics of Abortion*. Buffalo: Prometheus Books, 1993. Excerpts from court decisions such as *Roe v. Wade*, along with other opinionated readings from philosophers, ethicists, and activists.

Edward Batchelor Jr., ed., *Abortion: The Moral Issues*. New York: Pilgrim, 1982. A book of readings, especially concerned with the religious and ethical dimensions of the abortion question.

Marshall Cohen et al., eds., *The Rights and Wrongs of Abortion*. Princeton, NJ: Princeton University Press, 1974. Five rather technical philosophical essays about the ethics of abortion.

Celeste Michelle Condit, *Decoding Abortion Rhetoric*. Urbana: University of Illinois Press, 1990. An analysis of the words and images used by members of both sides of the abortion debate; special emphasis on the social forces affecting perspectives over the years.

Colin Francome, *Abortion Freedom: A Worldwide Movement*. London: George Allen and Unwin, 1984. A global perspective on abortion laws in various countries. Especially strong on the history of abortion rights and the ups and downs of the debate worldwide.

Thomas W. Hilgers et al., *New Perspectives on Human Abortion*. Frederick, MD: Aletheia Books, 1981. Readings on ethical, social, and biological factors influencing abortion in today's society. Very much written from an antiabortion perspective.

Alison Landes et al., eds., *Abortion: An Eternal Social and Moral Issue*. Wylie, TX: Information Plus, 1996. Explores the historical background and current public policy surrounding abortion. Includes many useful charts, graphs, and other statistics along with providing differing perspectives on some of the major controversies.

Kathleen McDonnell, *Not an Easy Choice*. Toronto: Women's, 1984. A feminist explores the importance of abortion in the women's movement. McDonnell concludes that abortion rights are vital but that the question is not as simple as some feminists would like to believe.

Periodicals

American Medical News, "ACOG Draws Fire for Saying Procedure 'May' Be Best Option for Some," March 3, 1997.

James Benedict, "The Use of Fetal Tissue," *Christian Century*, February 18, 1998.

Candace C. Crandall, "The Fetus Beat Us," *Women's Quarterly*, Winter 1996.

Gregg Easterbrook, "Medical Evolution: Will Homo Sapiens Become Obsolete?" *New Republic*, March 1, 1999.

Jeff Goldberg, "Fetal Attraction," *Discover*, July 1995.

Henry Goldman, "Sniper Kills Abortion Provider in N.Y.," *San Diego Union-Tribune*, October 25, 1998.

Jenny Hontz, "Twenty-Five Years Later: The Impact of *Roe v. Wade*," *Human Rights*, Spring 1998.

Alisdair Palmer, "We May Respect It—but We're Happy to Kill It," *Sunday Telegraph*, October 11, 1998.

David Rohde, "Three Abortion Doctors Secluded After Slaying," *San Diego Union-Tribune*, October 26, 1998.

Meredith Wadman, "Embryo Research Is Pro-Life," *New York Times*, February 21, 1996.

Washington Post National Weekly Edition, Paid advertisement, January 18, 1999.

Traci Watson, "A Tissue of Promises," *U.S. News & World Report*, August 8, 1994.

Internet Sources

"Abortion Advocate Admits Deception." www.prolife.org/rvw/ad1.html.

"Abortion Advocates Lie About Anesthesia." www.roevwade.org/advocates.html.

"Abortion Fact Sheet," 1995. www.christiananswers.net/summit/abrtfact.html.

"Abortion Foes Say They Won't Pay." www.choice.org/12. summaries.html.

American Academy of Pediatrics, "The Adolescent's Right to Confidential Care When Considering Abortion," May 1996. www.aap.org/policy/01348.html.

American Civil Liberties Union, "Stop Attacks on Reproductive Freedom." www.aclu.org/action/pba106.html.

American Pro-Life Network, "Statement on Violence." www.plnweb.com/violence.html.

Associated Press, "'Jane Roe' Goes Through Another Religious Conversion." www2.nando.net:80/newsroom/...01998/nation17_26582_noframes.html.

Baptist Message Online, "SBC Leaders Decry Recent Abortion Veto, Urge Clinton to Repent of Action," June 20, 1996. www.lacollege.edu/baptist/message/6.20.96/6.20.96/abortion.html.

Michael Bauman, "Verbal Plunder: Combating the Feminist Encroachment on the Language of Theology and Ethics," 1996. www.christiananswers.net/summit/plunder.html.

Linda Bevington, "Stem Cells and the Human Embryo: A Christian Analysis," February 5, 1999. www.bioethix.org/overviews/stemcell.html.

Jeff Builta, "Anti-Abortion Violence Movement Increases." www.acsp.uic.edu/oicj/pubs/cja/080603.htm.

Larry Frieders, "The New Abortionists: Chemical Abortion in Contemporary Culture." www.top.net/vitalsigns/vsmnewabort.html.

Carolyn Gargaro, "My Views as a Pro-Life Woman." www.gargaro.com/abortion.html.

———, "Protecting the Rights of Parents and Young Women—in Defense of the Child Custody Protection Act," June 12, 1998. www.gargaro.com/goodmanresponse.html.

Van Hilleary, "Hilleary Says Parental Consent for Abortion Is Necessary," September 2, 1997. www.house.gov/hilleary.

"Historical Abortion Beliefs of the Christian Church." www.religioustolerance.org/abo_hist.htm.

Dianne N. Irving, "NIH and Human Embryo Research Revisited: What Is Wrong with This Picture?" 1999. www.all.org/abac/dni002.htm

Brian Elroy McKinley, "Why Abortion is Biblical." www.elroy. com/ehr/abortion.html.

NARAL, "'Justifiable Homicide' and the Anti-Choice Movement." www.naral.org/publications/facts/shooting.html.

————, "So-Called 'Partial-Birth' Abortion Ban." www.naral.org/ issues/pba.html.

————, "Wisconsin Judge Rules Again." www.naral.org/publications/ press/98jun/061298.html.

"Parental Consent or Notification for Teen Abortions: Pro and Con." www.religioustolerance.org/abo_pare.htm.

"Partial Birth Abortion: Background Info." www.prolifeinfo.org/ pba.html.

"Partial Compassion," 1996. www.rcrc.org/pubs/speakout/lateterm. html.

"Past and Present Beliefs of the Christian Church." www. religioustolerance.org/abo_hist.htm.

"The Pro-Life Advocate." members.aol.com/pladvocate.

Pro-Life America, "Women Killed by Abortion." www.prolife. com/DEADWMN.html.

"Pro-Woman . . . Pro-Child . . . Pro-Peace." members.tripod.com/ ~lifepeace.

David C. Reardon, "Rape, Incest, and Abortion: Searching Beyond the Myths." www.prolife.org/afterabortion/rape.html.

"Refuse and Resist! Condemns Bombing." www.bodypolitic.org/ news/rr80130.htm.

Reproductive Health and Rights Center, "U.S. Premiere of Spanish Version of Fadiman Documentary." www.choice.org/12. summaries.html.

Pablo Rodriguez, "Testimony of Pablo Rodriguez, M.D." www. prochoice.org/violence/rodrig.htm.

"*Roe v. Wade*—Twenty-Five Years of Life Denied." www.roevwade. org/women.html.

Patricia Schrock, "Fetal Tissue Transplantation," Winter 1997. www.hsc.missouri.edu/~shrp/radsci/fetal/fetal.html.

Stephen Schwarz, "The Moral Question of Abortion," 1990. www. ohiolife.org/mqa/2-3.htm.

Marlena Sobel, "Abortion Myths," July 1994. www.berkshire.net/~ifas/fw/9407/myths.html.

Dorothy C. Wertz, "Human Embryonic Stem Cells: A Source of Organ Transplants," *Gene Letter*, February 1999. geneletter.org/0299/HumanEmbryonicStemCells.htm.

"Why Women Have Abortions." www.infinet.com/~life/stats/whyabort.htm.

Raymond A. Zwerin and Richard J. Shapiro, "Judaism and Abortion," 1996. www.rcrc.org/religion/es/comp.html.

Index

abortion drugs, 19
Ades, Claudia Crown, 67
adoption, 54
  better alternative than
    abortion, 44
  long waiting lists for, 53
AIDS, 6
Alabama, 52
Alzheimer's disease, 89
Ambrose, Saint, 28
American Academy of Family
  Physicians, 82
American Academy of
  Pediatrics, 80, 82
American Civil Liberties Union
  (ACLU), 70
American College of
  Obstetricians and
  Gynecologists (ACOG), 67, 68
American Law Institute (ALI),
  12, 13, 44
American Medical Association,
  12, 64, 82
American Society of
  Anesthesiologists, 62
amniocentesis, 48
antiabortion movement
  abortion seen as murder by,
    24, 54, 55
  because fetus is person, 25, 26
  because of religious
    teachings, 28
  regardless of size of fetus,
    26–27
  when fetus reaches certain

age, 10–11
  see also criminalization of
    abortion; partial-birth
    abortion; pro-life movement
Aquinas, Saint Thomas, 10
Aristotle, 33
Associated Press survey, 64
Augustine, Saint, 10

Bauman, Michael, 55
Bible, 27, 28, 33, 88
birth defects, 12, 55
  abortion justified by, 43,
    47–48
  abortion not justified by,
    56–57
  slippery slope arguments
    and, 57–58
Blackmun, Justice Harry, 14, 15
breast cancer
  increased risk of, through
    abortion, 20
  lack of evidence on, 21

California, 52, 73
  Supreme Court, 12
Callahan, J.C., 32
Callahan, Sydney, 26
Catholic Hospital Association
  of the United States and
  Canada, 28
child abuse rates, 52
childcare
  women still primarily
    responsible for, 42

Christianity, 28, 34, 88
  see also Lutheran Church;
  Protestant Church; Roman
  Catholic Church
Clinton, Bill, 64, 68–69
cloning, 32
Commission on Population and
  the American Future, 13
Constitution, U.S., 14
criminalization of abortion
  benefits of, 51, 53
  civil rights threatened by, 41
  clear moral message conveyed
    by, 51
  necessity for
    because fetus has rights, 50
  negative implications of, 37
    for women, 38, 42
  see also antiabortion
    movement; history of
    abortion

Declaration of Helsinki, 87
DNA, 32
Dornan, Robert K., 53
Down's syndrome, 56, 57

El Salvador, 45

Family Planning Perspectives
  (journal), 45
Faux, Marian, 79
Feldt, Gloria, 41
feminists, 14
Feminists for Life of America,
  54
fetal tissue research
  continuation of, is ethical,

94–95, 97
  because of potential
    treatment of illness, 92, 93
  encourages abortions, 88
  immorality of, 85, 89, 90
  as infringement of human
    rights, 87
  poor standards in, 86
  similarity of tissue transplant
    to organ donation and, 96
fetus
  age of, should determine
    abortion decision, 15–16
  pain experienced by, 30, 62
  definitions of, 30–32, 33, 35
  as person, 24–25, 54, 55
  as potential rather than actual
    human being, 30, 31, 54
  see also antiabortion
    movement; birth defects;
    fetal tissue research
Fitzsimmons, Ron, 63, 64

Gardner, Charles A., 35
Gargaro, Carolyn, 52, 55,
  72–73, 75
Goodman, Ellen, 67
Gordon, Linda, 33
Gray, Nellie, 58
Gregory XIV (pope), 11
Guatemala, 45

Haskell, Martin, 62, 64
Hawaii, 13
Henshaw, Stanley, 78
Hilleary, Van, 73
history of abortion, 8–10
  changing attitudes and, 11–12

polarization of debate and, 8,
16–17
language of, 17–18
likely to continue, 21
twentieth-century laws and,
12–14
see also legalization of abortion
Hitler, Adolf, 57

incest, 46, 47
Indiana, 81
Innocent III (pope), 10–11
intact dilation and evacuation
(D&E)
is correct name for partial-
birth abortion, 66
is occasionally necessary, 67,
68
need for continuing legality of,
71
woman's wish for, should be
respected, 69–70
see also partial-birth abortion
Irving, Dianne N., 57, 86

Jefferson, Thomas, 7
Jerome, Saint, 10, 11
Judaism, 33, 34, 45

Kansas, 13, 45
Koop, C. Everett, 45
Kost, Kathryn, 78

legalization of abortion, 51
as civil right, 39–41
for poor as well as rich
women, 13
desensitization and, 58

encourages selfishness, 52
justifiable in certain cases,
44–45
including birth defects,
47–48
including rape and incest,
46–47
justified by tradition, 33–34
women's rights and, 41–42
see also parental consent laws;
Roe v. Wade
Lutheran Church, 45

Mahkorn, Sandra, 56
Maryland, 45
Massachusetts, 81
Mathewes-Green, Frederica, 54
McCorvey, Norma, 14
McDonnell, Kathleen, 26, 39,
41, 53
McMahon, James, 64
media, 6
Mill, John Stuart, 6
Minnesota, 74, 79, 81
miscarriage
fetal tissue from, not useful for
research, 88
Mississippi, 79, 82
Mother Teresa, 52, 53

National Abortion Federation,
63
National Coaljtion of Abortion
Providers, 63
National Institutes of Health
(NIH), 97
New Jersey, 13, 45, 64
New York, 13

abortion banned in, 11
abortion legalized in, 14
Nicholson, Susan, 46

organ donations, 96

parental consent laws
  dangers of, due to delay in
    timing of abortion, 81
  dangers of, in dysfunctional
    families, 78–79
  family relationships ignored
    by, 80
  family strengthened by, 72, 73
  incidence of teen abortion
    reduced by, 74
  incidence of teen abortion not
    reduced by, 82
  rights and safety of teens
    compromised by, 82
  safeguards in, 76
  teen health protected by, 75
Parkinson's disease, 97
  fetal tissue research and,
    85–86, 92–93
partial-birth abortion, 17–18, 61
  brutality of, 62, 65
  given reasons for, do not
    justify, 64
  numbers of, 63
  see also intact dilation and
    evacuation (D&E)
Pennsylvania, 76
Pius IX (pope), 12
Planned Parenthood, 41, 63
Plato, 33
pregnancy, 31, 40
  as handicap in workplace,

41–42
  not only woman's concern, 54
  risks of abortion for women
    and, 9–10, 52
  reduction of, 15
pro-choice movement, 17
  partial-birth abortion and, 63,
    64, 67, 69
  reasons for choosing abortion
    and, 38
  seriousness of, 39
pro-life movement, 17, 18, 39,
  58, 95
  biased literature of, 70
  children's lives saved by, 51
  exceptions should be allowed
    by, 45, 46
  history ignored by, 32–34
  intensification of illegal
    protests by, 19
  on link between abortion and
    breast cancer, 20–21
  misleading name of, 66
Protestant Church, 11, 14
  see also Christianity

Quindlen, Anna, 37

rape, 8, 12, 46
  does not justify abortion,
    55–56
  small number of abortion
    cases resulting from, 45
Rashi (Jewish scholar), 33
right-to-life movement. See
  pro-life movement
Roe v. Wade, 14, 16, 37, 38,
  57–58

abortion legal and advertised
under, 51
women given constitutional
right to abortion by, 16
Roman Catholic Church, 14,
28, 34
abortion accepted by,
historically, 10–11
abortion banned by, in
nineteenth century, 12
RU-486, 19

Schwarz, Stephen, 27
Shinn, Roger L., 40
Sloan, Don, 38
Southern Baptist Church, 45,
61
Supreme Court, U.S., 14, 15,
72

teenagers, 69
under pressure, 6

see also parental consent laws
Tennessee, 81
Tertullian, 28
Texas, 14
original abortion law in, 34
Thomson, Judith Jarvis, 40
Twain, Mark, 6

United States, 34
anti-immigrant sentiment in,
11
murder common in, 50

Virginia, 79

Warren, Mary Anne, 31
Washington, D.C., 12–13
Watts, Tammy, 68
Wertheimer, Roger, 25
Wisconsin, 13
women's rights, 55
see also Roe v. Wade

ABOUT THE AUTHOR

Stephen Currie is the author of forty books and many magazine articles. Among his nonfiction titles are *Birthday a Day, Life in a Wild West Show*, and *We Have Marched Together: The Working Children's Crusade*. He has also written *Slavery* in Greenhaven's Opposing Viewpoints Digest series. He lives in upstate New York with his wife, Amity, and his children Irene and Nicholas.